MAKERS IN SCHOOLS

Entering the Fourth Industrial Revolution

EDITED BY
SUSAN BROWN &
BARBARA LIEDAHL

Makers in Schools: Entering the Fourth Industrial Revolution
Edited by Susan Brown & Barbara Liedahl

Published by EduMatch®
PO Box 150324, Alexandria, VA 22315
www.edumatch.org

© 2018 Susan Brown & Barbara Liedahl
All rights reserved. No portion of this book may be reproduced in any form without permission from the publisher, except as permitted by U.S. copyright law. For permissions contact sarah@edumatch.org.

These books are available at special discounts when purchased in quantities of more than 10 for use as premiums, promotions fundraising, and educational use. For inquiries and details, contact the publisher: sarah@edumatch.org.

TABLE OF CONTENTS

Foreword by Jaime Donally 1
Section I: Introducing Makerspaces 5
    Maker Mindset in Education: Susan Brown 7
    Infusing the Maker Mindset Across A District:
    Traci Bonde 29
    Maker PD: Jacie Maslyk 37
    The Learning Laboratory: Michael Terborg 61
Section II: Makerspaces in Specific Settings 81
    "Making" it Happen: Keri Hennessy-Wilson 83
    Makerspace and English Language Learners:
    Clara Alaniz 93
    MAKE-ing the Most of the Curriculum:
    Jennifer Bond 103
    Converging STEAM Technologies: Ella Marie 117
    The Classroom or Library as a Makerspace:
    Jackie Gerstein, Ed.D 133
Section III: 153
Practical Ideas for Makerspaces in Education 153
    Bring the Maker Movement to Your School:
    Barbara Liedahl 155
    Making Something Out of Nothing:
    Brian Costello 171
    From Storyboard to Silver Screen:
    Debbie Bohanan 185
    Green Screens as Makerspaces: Martine Brown 195
    Go Green: Michael DuBose 203
    Color Me Happy: Katie J. McNamara 215
    Addendum (Where Shall We Go from Here?) 223

FOREWORD

Jaime Donally

The times of creativity confined to a single location is a thing of the past. Don't get me wrong, makerspaces are incredible, but to think that innovation requires a perfectly planned space that has an assortment of supplies and includes all the top gadgets is absurd. Our students can demonstrate knowledge in a variety of ways, and "making" is an option that should be available with or without a makerspace.

Looking back at my personal educational journey, I've always tended to be creative in the way that I learn. I'm inclined to jump in head first when given the freedom to showcase my knowledge in a non-traditional project such as art or technology. When given a strict guidance in a lesson, I do the minimum required to get the maximum grade, but when given an open door, I excel beyond the expectations, because I'm given the freedom to do so.

The desire to give our students this same freedom is the reason behind one of my projects I started a few years back called Global Maker Day. I had already been involved with global collaboration for both educators and students, but I felt like each event was a repeat of the same information shared, but there was no significant change taken place from one event to the next. I would leave the events wishing for a way to combine the global collaboration and action to truly impact the classroom, thus the beginning of #GlobalMakerDay.

The annual event is full of presentation from educators, students, whole classrooms and companies sharing ways they "make" and while showcasing the amazing things they are doing, they're challenging the participants to create along with them. The individual presenters who have been part of Global Maker Day have unbelievable talent, but something very special took us all by surprise from the beginning. While giving the students a chance to create and share what they've made during the challenges, we were in awe to see the posts on Twitter exhibiting innovation at its finest. Not one post looked the same. Each student took the challenge in a different direction and each represented the individuality of the students' interest and passion.

I left the first event recognizing that Global Maker Day wasn't about finding the correct answer or solving a problem correctly, but it opened the floodgates of possibility. What can our students do if given the opportunity? After getting a glimpse of the spotlight on our students for that short time, I was hooked. Global Maker Day wasn't about a single day or a single event, it's about transformation. Our classroom lessons need to change, our approach needs to adjust, our connections need an upgrade, we need a revolution of remaking for all students.

Of course, immediately after these events, we're getting correspondence from educators sharing that students are asking when they get to do this again. They want to have Global Maker Day every day, and I agree. I hope that Global Maker Day inspires change that extends beyond the day and into the regular classroom experiences.

Fast forward 30+ years, I still don't get as many opportunities as I prefer to showcase my creative ideas mainly due to my own time limitations. When I do block out the time, I'm immediately rejuvenated and have increased confidence that I can accomplish anything. Regularly challenging myself is necessary for growth, and I hope to continue to grow professionally through maker activities.

I'm honored to be connected with so many other makers who push the classroom forward through innovative ideas. The contributors in this book will inspire many educators to consider ways to invite creativity into their classroom through maker projects. Don't forget to include your students as you adapt your classroom to be an innovation hub and don't forget to use the #GlobalMakerDay hashtag in your posts so we can highlight and share with others!

Section I: Introducing Makerspaces

The next four chapters are all about introducing makerspaces into our schools. We need to start somewhere, and the maker mindset sets the stage, empowering educators to guide their students to pursue a path of learning that is meaningful to them. Addressing a shifting culture in today's classrooms, we look to scaling up and infusing this vision in a classroom, in a school, and even in a district. You will find in these chapters why active, hands-on professional development focusing on the creative process and passion-driven learning is significant. Lastly, we look to where this learning can happen in unexpected settings.

- **Maker Mindset in Education** by Susan Brown
- **Infusing the Maker Mindset Across A District** by Traci Bonde
- **Maker PD** by Jacie Maslyk
- **The Learning Laboratory** by Michael Terborg

MAKER MINDSET IN EDUCATION

Susan Brown

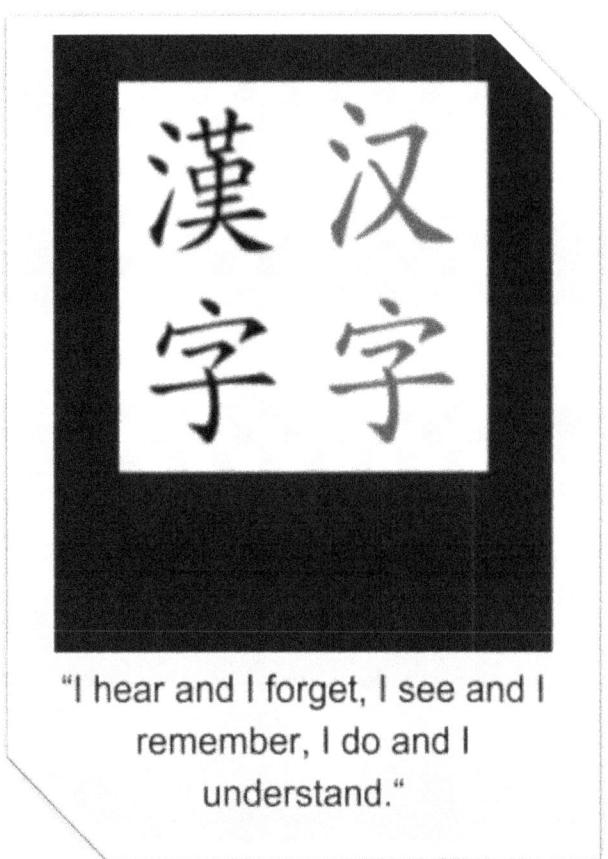

"I hear and I forget, I see and I remember, I do and I understand."

Definition: Maker Mindset

Make Magazine's Dale Dougherty defines as "what can you do with what you know?"

MAKERS IN SCHOOLS:
ENTERING THE FOURTH INDUSTRIAL REVOLUTION

Definition: Maker Pedagogy

According to Shawn Bullock, maker pedagogy

is an approach that utilizes the principles of ethical **hacking** (i.e., deconstructing existing technology for the purpose of creating knowledge), **adapting** (i.e., the freedom to use a technology for new purposes), **designing** (i.e., selecting components and ideas to solve problems), and **creating** (i.e., archiving contextual knowledge obtained through engaging in the process of making, as well as the actual tangible products) as part of an overall way of working with those interested in learning about science and technology (Bullock, 2014).

Definition: Disruptive Innovation

a term of art coined by Clayton Christensen which describes a process by which a product or service takes root initially in simple applications at the bottom of a market and then relentlessly moves up market, eventually displacing established competitors.

Why I chose to become a disruptive innovator in education

I started teaching late in my career. I wanted to be in the teaching profession from early on, but avoided earning a teaching degree when I was in college. Why? I grew up participating in a youth organization that uses hands-on, project-based learning as its educational philosophy. When I finally did join the public school system, first as a parent volunteer, then aide, then teacher, media specialist and now, in Central Office as an Instructional Specialist, I brought with me that hands-on learning philosophy and tried to apply it in classrooms, whenever possible.

Then, in 2013, two things happened: first, my friend and colleague, Barbara Liedahl, invited me to learn to add interactivity to my artwork. Too cool! Secondly, that same friend, who continues to lead me down the path of discovery, told me about Makerspaces. Ideas began percolating so fast, my head was spinning. *So, there was* a way to bring Jean Piaget, Vygotsky, Seymour Papert and their theories of Constructivism and Constructionism, into the classroom. The classroom I was looking to change at the time was the school-library classroom. Keep the books, but add space to include 21st-century technologies. Basically, give children hands-on activities that explore high-low technologies, in a non-tested area, so they might use what they know and build on it, standing on the shoulders of giants.

Why change? Why now?

As I type this introductory chapter using the newest version of G Suite's Google Docs, I include interactive links, to add depth and breadth to my ideas. The book will be published as an electronic book so that the reader might follow those links. I hope that we will be able to allow readers to respond to other's thoughts and ideas, via comments in some Google doc-like manner, and if you are online reading this, new vocabulary words and ideas can be defined in a few clicks of the trackpad. I also hope you are accessing this from some digital tool that affords you that interactivity. At the very least, I hope you have the ability to follow me to places I have discovered that inspire me. Many of you will. Using these and a myriad of digital communication innovations is leading us into the next Industrial Revolution.

Change is happening faster and faster in the world around us, but pedagogy seems to be stuck in the past. Why? We need to realize that much of the world is still living with vestiges of the 1st and 2nd Industrial Ages, characterized in part by the development of the steam engine and the factory system, the telegraph and later, telephones and TV, and synthetic resources, like plastics. Why? And why have we taken the hands-on, minds-on approach to teaching and learning out? Can we recapture the old shop and home-economics classroom approach in a high-low tech manner? Why are we struggling so with where and how technology appears in the curriculum? Doesn't a maker mindset support what today's employers require of a prospective hire? Let's look back to the beginning of what is, at present, the model for our education system. It was midway between the 1st and 2nd Industrial Revolutions that the structure of our present system was developed. What and how we teach was developed during these industrial ages. I would like to defer to Dr. Ioannis Miaoulis, president of the Boston Science Museum. In his 2010 National Center for Technological Literacy STEM speech, he explains that:

> The topics that we teach now were decided by the Committee of Ten, actually at Harvard University, back in 1893.

The Committee of Ten followed a very rational process: they looked at what kids learned at home, they decided what kids should know when they graduate from high school, either to enter the workforce or to enter University, and they came up with the topics that cover the gap between what kids learned at home and what kids should know when they graduate. So disciplines such as Physics and Chemistry and Biology came into the curriculum but Technology was left out. Back in 1893, most children were growing up on farms and most technology was farming technology, so kids were learning technology at home on the farm, so it wasn't necessary for the topic of Technology and Engineering to be part of the mainstream curriculum.

Our school's curriculum was developed 125 years ago. Time to change, don't you think? Maybe it is time to change our focus from, as he stated later in the speech, that we should be studying more of the human-made world. So maybe the question is: Do we need to study and experience more of the human-made world using hands-on, minds-on learning, somewhere in our schooling? Don't we need to take our students with us? Not as "Guide on the Side," but "Guide on the Ride"?

Now reflect on J. Robert Oppenheimer's quote from a speech he delivered at the closing of the Columbia University Bicentennial Anniversary celebration, December 26, 1964:

MAKERS IN SCHOOLS:
ENTERING THE FOURTH INDUSTRIAL REVOLUTION

> One thing that is new is the prevalence of newness, the changing scale and scope of change itself, so that the world alters as we walk in it, so that the years of man's life measure not some small growth or rearrangement or moderation of what he learned in childhood, but a great upheaval.

We are in the midst of that great upheaval, every day, every hour, every minute, every second... ever-present change. Do we, living in this "advanced" society, continue to leave the human technologies out of the classroom? How do we, as teachers, keep up with today's technology? How do we guide them in ways that will help students retain what they have learned, past test-taking time? Can we use that study of the human-made world *and* integrate language arts, math, social studies, and the arts? How do we teach where the students live now... in a physical AND digital world?

Sir Ken Robinson speaks elegantly about how our education system developed, illustrating the link between the factory model and our present-day school systems. There are theories and arguments across the board that beg to change how and what we teach, the idea of Growth Mindset, for example. The World Economic Forum's take on a Fourth Industrial Revolution is a powerful example. Jeremy Rifkin, world-renowned social and economic theorist, says we are entering into the Third Industrial Revolution and begs us to change, to adjust to what he calls the Internet of Things (IoT). He defines IoT as the coming together of three huge technological changes:

- First, the World Wide Web.
- Secondly, the development of renewable energy from our sun and wind.
- Lastly, automation of transportation; such as driverless road, rail and air transportation of goods and services.

Rifkin's economic models not only describe the change that is needed but document it, as parts of Europe and China have already begun the transformation that will impact what and how we teach. The *STEM Education Act of 2015* (H.R. 1020) signed into law under the Obama Administration and the development of Computer Science curriculum for K-12 show that we are dipping our pedagogical toes into the oceans of needed change. Google (the verb) "skills for today's workforce" and you will discover, again, the National Education Association's (NEA) "An Educator's Guide to the "Four Cs":

- Communication
- Collaboration
- Creativity
- Critical thinking.

I am going out on a limb and saying all of these ideas, theories, beliefs support the need to bring hands-on, maker mindset learning "back to the future!"

Let's look at how some educators and education philosophies might guide us. Mitchel Resnick, Professor at the MIT Media Lab and developer of Scratch software, writes in his Aug. 2016 Design Blog:

We know that kids will become most engaged, and learn the most when they are working on projects that are personally meaningful to them. But no single project will be meaningful to all kids. So, if we want to engage *all* kids—from many different backgrounds, with many different interests—we need to support a wide diversity of pathways and projects.

His Lifelong Kindergarten research group at the MIT Media Lab says;

The kindergarten approach to learning - characterized by a spiraling cycle of Imagine, Create, Play, Share, Reflect, and back to Imagine - is ideally suited to the needs of the 21st century, helping learners develop the creative-thinking skills that are critical to success and satisfaction in today's society.

Sylvia Martinez and Gary Stagers's book, *Invent to Learn: Making, Tinkering, and Engineering in the Classroom,* echoes the ideas of Seymour Papert and his ideas that took Piaget's Constructivism to Constructionism, "where knowledge occurs best through building things that are concrete and shareable." The teacher role becomes a facilitator who coaches and helps students in attaining their own goals as reported by Martinez and Stager in their book.

John Spencer, a professor of instructional technology, explains in his YouTube video "The Shift from Engaging Students to Empowering Learners" that his goal is to teach teachers to create a learning environment that supports students to move from "compliance to engaged", where they "want to learn rather than have to learn." I subscribe to his YouTube channel and use his brilliance all the time.

A core component of the Montessori Method "is based on self-directed activity, hands-on learning, and collaborative play." In Montessori classrooms, children make creative choices in their learning, while the classroom and the teacher offer age-appropriate activities to guide the process.

A famous Montessori graduate, Temple Grandin, American professor of animal science at Colorado State University, and consultant to the livestock industry on animal behavior was diagnosed with autism as a child. She talks about how her mind works in TED Ed's "Temple Grandin: The World Needs All Kinds of Thinkers": and explains, from the view of an autism activist:

> The normal brain ignores the details. Well, if you're building a bridge, details are pretty important because it'll fall down if you ignore the details. And one of my big concerns with a lot of policy things today is things are getting too abstract. People are getting away from doing hands-on stuff. I'm really concerned that a lot of the schools have taken out the hands-on classes, because art and classes like that -- those are the classes where I excelled.

Circle back to Mitch Resnick's quote:

MAKERS IN SCHOOLS:
ENTERING THE FOURTH INDUSTRIAL REVOLUTION

But no single project will be meaningful to all kids. So, if we want to engage *all* kids—from many different backgrounds, with many different interests—we need to support a wide diversity of pathways and projects.

This philosophy is nearly impossible to accomplish in a factory model of education, but as factories move humans to managers in an automated assembly line, perhaps we can imagine and develop a system that allows students to become managers of their own learning, and teachers become guides to support student's management and learning (metacognition?) skills.

So, let's look at how we use "human-made" technology in our classrooms? How do we integrate technology into the curriculum? Teach the students to type? Does a technology class consist only of learning to use Word, Excel, PowerPoint, a desktop, laptop, cloud technology, smartphones? Do we use these as tools to teach more? Where do we teach them to use YouTube for purposes that will support a creative, productive life? How do we use technology to give students choice, engage them, help them fall in love with learning?

We must remember that technology does not refer only to digital technology. Without the invention of the printing press, the digital revolution could not have occurred. The tools that continue to be invented or reinvented are taking us from analog to digital. As many of us in education are still struggling with the digital revolution, MIT's Neil Gershenfeld said in his 2008 Ted Talk, and I paraphrase to some extent, yes, we have had a "digital revolution, but I'd like to argue that it's done; we won. We've had a digital revolution, but we don't need to keep having it." So where should we be taking our students then? What's next in this "great upheaval" already happening all around us. It is already here, in Makerspaces across the world. Combining analog and digital, or physical computing; it is already a thing.

Tom Igoe helps define this new "digital" revolution, touching our lives in every way imaginable, from measuring weight gain of a beehive as pollen and nectar are collected and sending that info to an app on my phone, to collecting heart rate and oxygen use data as a marathon runner sprints to finish line. In manufacturing, you see evidence of physical computing in your new Samsung fridge that tells you what's in it, or your Apple Siri turning down the lights at your request. But the sensors and actuators that are listening/watching and then following your directions are being controlled by a microcontroller, or many microcontrollers, talking between themselves to make things happen. The languages they use will be taught in school. Why? Because, now, we are taking analog machines and adding digital interactive systems to make life easier, better, etc. But the analog technology remains. We use a hammer, a needle, and thread, and if we take Merriam Webster's definition of analog (see 2a) I would say that humans are analog... at least for now. Digital will not replace analog for the most part, though movies and TV might lead us to believe otherwise. Just give us more choices. So, what does this have to do with Makerspaces in Schools?

Sylvia Martinez and Gary Stager in a 2013 article write:

MAKERS IN SCHOOLS:
ENTERING THE FOURTH INDUSTRIAL REVOLUTION

The Maker Movement is a technological and creative revolution underway around the world. Fortunately for educators, the Maker Movement overlaps with the natural inclinations of children and the power of learning by doing. Embracing the lessons of the Maker Movement holds the keys to reanimating the best, but oft-forgotten learner-centered teaching practices. New tools and technology, such as 3D printing, robotics, microprocessors, wearable computing, e-textiles, "smart" materials, and new programming languages are being invented at an unprecedented pace. The Maker Movement creates affordable -- even free -- versions of these inventions, and shares tools and ideas online creating a vibrant, collaborative community of global problem-solvers.

My learning process

So, I mentioned that Barbara had invited me to learn about using conductive thread to create a Valentine pin that could light up. Ok, that was cool. We ended up at our friend Ginny's house with another friend, Dee, a Library Media Specialist. So here I am, sewing, learning about circuits (a 5th-grade science topic), next to an elementary school library media specialist, across from Ginny, my instructional tech mentor, and Barbara, an Instructional Specialist. Dee's principal loved the idea of bringing hands-on project-based learning to a population of students that lived, for the most part, in low-income households that spoke Spanish, English,

Korean, French, Farsi, and other languages at home. So now we are teaching kids the vocabulary of sewing... thread, not string; needle, not pokey thing; and tried almost in vain, to teach them to spell the word sew (so, suw, sow, soo...) We were in the infancy of having them write about what they had created and the process.

So (lol), here are some of the innovations that have helped us build past just struggling to get the needle threaded, and the blanket stitch right:

- Growth Mindset and the ability to help students *AND* ourselves understand how this affects us throughout our lives.
- Google Classroom: We can add YouTube videos to allow them to learn at their own pace.
- Google Docs:
    - We can assign a template that asks them to document their progress and/or process including:
        - Materials used
        - Areas of ease/challenge
        - Things to do differently
        - Including a snapshot
    - They can take a snapshot of their progress right from their Chromebook.

- Google Drive: All of the assignments are stored both in the associated Google Classroom AND in the student's own Google Drive. Thus, they are creating a portfolio of work, hopefully showing development of their reasoning, problem-solving, persistence, resilience, as well as their writing, photography, and organizational skills.

Maybe not an innovation, but working with vendors and giving them feedback helps keep everyone in the loop. Loops include prices, their innovations, our needs, and wants, what works for us, what works for them. Doesn't always help, but every voice counts. We keep telling one of our favorite vendors to drop the price on a certain item so we could afford to buy more of what really counts. So far, we know they are at least talking about it.

This, too, is not so much of an innovation as a must do: inclusion at all levels of ability. Our talented and gifted students need to discover that failure is not an enemy, as they create the first paper circuit and it doesn't light. And I must share one of my favorite 2 minutes in my teaching career: One of our after-school makers, a fifth grader, special ed with no English at home, comes to me all excited. "Mrs. Brown, Mrs. Brown, guess what I got on my science test!" I think; "Gosh, he wouldn't be bragging about a C..." so I look at him with a big smile and say; B? "No!" he says; "I got an A!" "Wow! What was the test on?" I ask, thinking it would be some easy science concept. "Circuits!" he says. I ask him what kinds of questions he had to answer. Let me tell you folks, had we not been learning about paper circuits from Jie Qi's awesome web tutorials, and Leah Buechley's e-textile guides, I wouldn't have been able to answer those questions!

And then there are the "newcomers" to our country. So many are English Language Learners. Check out Clara J. Alaniz's great chapter, "Makerspace and English Language Learners." Keri Hennessy-Wilson's chapter, too. We shared many of the same experiences and goals: starting an after-school makerspace to integrate making into an everyday classroom norm.

Where we plan to go

Barbara and I are working a team to develop a course called "Transforming Education Thru Maker Movement" This course will give teachers the continuing education we all need and will be equal to 3 graduate credits. We presented Barbara's Makerspace in a Box idea (see chapter 7) to the technology team two years ago, and they loved it. To help bring more of their teachers on board, our wonderful team wrote a proposal to develop this first level of Maker Mindset, that includes hands-on activities they can use with their classrooms.

And by the way, I finally realized that one of our authors, Jackie Gerstein, Ed.D, is the author we have been quoting quite a bit in this course. She has impacted the course in very important ways. See her chapter, "The Classroom or Library as a Makerspace."

I also want to give a shout out to my friend, Dr. Ella Marie. We tested a huge amount of the curriculum we are developing, using her 8th-grade science classes. I will let her tell the story, chapter 13. And the curriculum writing? See Jennifer Bond's "MAKE-ing the Most of the Curriculum" and

MAKERS IN SCHOOLS:
ENTERING THE FOURTH INDUSTRIAL REVOLUTION

all administrators will want to read Traci Bonde's "Infusing the Maker Mindset Across A District."

The next two sections of this book, featuring Martine Brown, Debbie Bohanan, Brian Costello, Michael DuBose, Katie McNamara, and my genius friend, Barbara, take us right into the making!

Where I would like to see our schools go

What if the school library was a place for students to find resources, analog and digital, plus the tools and materials to create? Even if we started with rulers, scissors that actually cut, big rolls of paper, cardboard boxes, string, and crayons, the students could make models of simple machines. Perfect 3rd-grade fun! What if, by 4th and 5th-grade they were adding circuits to a box that used simple machines to function as, say, a Martian Rover? Then they could power LED lights to light the way for filming the landscape.

What if there were LEGOs? What if there were tablet stands for the students to hold an iPad while filming a presentation on how they made a circuit to power that Martian Rover lighting system? What if the students had to request materials as they came up with a design, measured, and listed the tools and materials they needed? What if directions and tutorials were curated and uploaded to a teacher-librarian's Google Classroom? What if, by doing this, we were teaching our students to use YouTube purposefully and positively. What if this method allowed students to work at their own pace? What if they could document their progress, their growth (persistence, skill, resilience) in their Google Drive by way of assignments in Google Classroom?

What if students shared their progress with other students to get ideas, feedback, help to make their ideas work?

What if students could share all this with their parents? What if the teacher-librarians shared their Google Classrooms with classroom teachers? What if there were enough hours of professional development to support those teacher-librarians to build their teaching skills to include these ideas? See Jacie Maslyk's "Maker PD: Active Professional Learning That Sparks Creativity." Spicing up staff develop brings teacher engagement and enthusiasm on par with our students! Jacie hits the nail on the head!

My vision isn't new. It has been developing over the past 5 years, pulling from the Makerspace Playbook School Edition, Mary Cay Ricci, friend and author of the New York Times' best-seller education book, *Mindsets in the Classroom* introducing me to Growth Mindset, John Spencer and A.J. Juliani, and more than anything, my experience growing up in 4-H.

I need to say a little about 4-H. I learned to make stuff. From chocolate cakes and apple pies, to insect collections and wooden boxes. I learned to sew. I learned to use craft materials.

But I also learned to demonstrate what I had learned. I learned to write about what I was learning. I learned to help others learn what I had learned. I didn't get grades, but there were competitions. I didn't win the biggest prize most of the time, but I did my best. When I won a ribbon that wasn't as good as I would have liked, I tried again. I didn't fail. I figured out what I did wrong, or how I could do it better, or practiced getting better.

I realize that there is no way to give a number grade to provide data to a chocolate cake that didn't have enough baking powder, so it didn't rise enough, but made really darn good brownies. Now they won the champion brownie ribbon that year. So, what does baking a cake show? It shows that at 11 years old, I could measure, I could read a recipe, I could ask for help (Grandmother, does this really say a ¼ teaspoon or should that t be a T?). I learned about the ingredients and the tools, about how to spell them, what they did in the mixture or what they were used for to bake a cake. I learned to tell the funny story about the chocolate cake I finally made coming in second to my brownies at the county fair.

But that was back in the '60s. My mom was a stay-at-home mom. I was not. She and my dad were married and together. I was a single mom. My parents took the time to take us places, like the 4-H events, and more. I was working full-time and working on the next certification/ degree. So, though I tried to raise my boys in 4-H as well, theirs' was a whole different experience. I just didn't have time. I am not feeling sorry for myself. I am describing so many families today. Society has changed so much. Oppenheimer's "*scale and scope of change itself*" is only beginning to rear it's snowballing head. Many of you reading this already know the necessity of hands-on learning.

So how do we begin to provide that experience in schools, all schools? I don't have the answer. I do know that I will keep the Frank Sinatra song, High Hopes, playing in my head. How about you?

References

An Educator's Guide to the "Four Cs". (n.d.). Retrieved June 07, 2018, from http://www.nea.org/tools/52217.htm

Buechley, L. (n.d.). Sew Electric. Retrieved August 19, 2018, from http://sewelectric.org/about/

Bullock, S. (2015, May 24). What is maker pedagogy? Retrieved August 26, 2018, from http://makerpedagogy.org/en/what-is-maker-pedagogy-some-early-thoughts/

Christensen, C. (2012, October 23). Disruptive Innovation. Retrieved August 26, 2018, from http://www.claytonchristensen.com/key-concepts/

Core Components of Montessori Education. (n.d.). Retrieved April 20, 2018, from https://amshq.org/Montessori-Education/Introduction-to-Montessori/Core-Components-of-Montessori-Education

Dougherty, D., Hlubinka, M., Thomas, P., Chang, S., Hoefer, S., Alexander, I., & McGuire, D. (2013, Spring). Makerspace Playbook - Maker Education Initiative - Every ... Retrieved April 18, 2018, from https://makered.org/wp-content/uploads/2014/09/Makerspace-Playbook-Feb-2013.pdf

Gershenfeld, N. (2006). Unleash your creativity in a Fab Lab. Retrieved April 18, 2018, from http://www.ted.com/talks/neil_gershenfeld_on_fab_labs

S. (2010, August 09). High Hopes - Frank Sinatra. Retrieved from https://www.youtube.com/watch?v=eWR3IkfHdLE

Igoe, T. (2004, June 4). What Is Physical Computing? [Web log post]. Retrieved April 18, 2018, from http://www.tigoe.com/blog/what-is-physical-computing/

J. Robert Oppenheimer. (2013). Retrieved January 07, 2018, from http://www.worldhistory.biz/sundries/33278-j-robert-oppenheimer.html

Juliani, A. J. (2017, June 07). Forget Guide on the Side...Students Need a Guide on the Ride. Retrieved August 20, 2017, from http://ajjuliani.com/forget-guide-side-students-need-guide-ride/

Miaoulis, I. (n.d.). Ioannis Miaoulis NCTL STEM Speech. Speech presented at National Center for Technological Literacy STEM, Boston. Retrieved June 26, 2014, from https://www.youtube.com/watch?v=4B-g1_6QCWU

Mitchel Resnick: Designing for Wide Walls. (2017, July 18). Retrieved January 07, 2018, from https://design.blog/2016/08/25/mitchel-resnick-designing-for-wide-walls/

Oppenheimer, J. R. (1984). Uncommon Sense. Retrieved January 07, 2018, from https://books.google.com/books?id=o0jUBwAAQBAJ

Qi, J. (n.d.). About. Retrieved August 17, 2018, from http://technolojie.com/about/

Qi, J. (n.d.). How-to. Retrieved August 19, 2018, from https://chibitronics.com/how-to-page/

Ricci, M. C. (2017). Mindsets in the classroom: Building a culture of success and student achievement in schools. Waco, TX: Prufrock Press.

Sir Ken Robinson Talks About Factory-Like Education. (2014, March 17). Retrieved July 07, 2018, from https://www.youtube.com/watch?v=K9C0KNtqiHU

Spencer, J. (2017, June 09). The Shift from Engaging Students to Empowering Learners. Retrieved June 14, 2017, from https://www.youtube.com/watch?v=BYBJQ5rIFjA

The Third Industrial Revolution: A Radical New Sharing Economy. (2018, February 13). Retrieved April 18, 2018, from https://www.youtube.com/watch?v=QX3M8Ka9vUA

World Economic Forum. (2015, December 17). The Fourth Industrial Revolution. Retrieved April 18, 2018, from https://www.youtube.com/watch?v=SCGV1tNBoeU

About the Author

With a BS in Agriculture, certified to teach K-8, Masters in Instructional Technology, and Admin Certification, Susan believes that her youth spent as a 4-Her was a major influence on her hands-on, project/problem-based, constructivist perspective. An Instructional Technology Specialist, Susan works with school librarians across the school district, with the goal of changing the face of school libraries. She has facilitated workshops at ISTE and other National, State, and Regional Conferences supporting the Maker Mindset, Arts Integration, STEAM, and Technology Integration.

INFUSING THE MAKER MINDSET ACROSS A DISTRICT

Traci Bonde

In January 2015, I was appointed as the first Chief Technology Officer for Dublin Unified School District. It is located in the Bay Area in California and has approximately 11,500 students. I have been the first in many new positions in many roles throughout my career. What I have discovered is when you are the first in a newly created position, you have a great responsibility and opportunity to forge the framework and the path for what that position may ultimately look like. Many of us know that job descriptions never define our work. That held true in this great opportunity to infuse the maker mindset across all elements of the school district.

Now I'll begin by making the first statement; we are not a maker district. We have no school that can claim to be 100% a maker school. What we have rather, is a shift in culture as a result of an introduction to the maker movement as a mindset. I am a firm believer that the maker movement is a mindset, rather than a station or a library destination. The spirit of innovation, creativity, collaboration, drive the mindset that encourages both our students and staff to take risks, to be innovative, to explore improving the world around them.

Within the first five months of my position, I had taken my entire team to the Friday MakerFaire Education day. It gave my team a chance to immerse themselves in the MakerFaire movement and better understand what I meant when I said, we are all makers. No one on my team in the

MAKERS IN SCHOOLS:
ENTERING THE FOURTH INDUSTRIAL REVOLUTION

Technology Services Department had ever heard of or had ever been to a MakerFaire event. I will tell you that for at least three of my staff, it changed their work significantly. What had been a mindset in the Department of Technology support which consisted of answering tech tickets troubleshooting issues with software and hardware and responding to fires slowly begin to shift to the department that they are today.

    I am proud to say, my team, today has some of the most innovative technology professionals that I have ever led. They often look at a problem now as an opportunity to recycle, refresh, and begin anew with everything from the infrastructure to the cabling to the mounting of a TV to the placement of items on a presentation cart to the way that students are introduced to technology on their Chromebooks. Another staff person in my department built a makerspace at home so that he could tinker and explore when not at work. Several of the members of my department have become highly specialized in components of the MakerFaire movement and are co-teaching and presenting as a result of this exposure. This has been my most significant infiltration of a change effort moving a district toward the maker mindset to date.

Another angle I began tackling as early as January 2015 as I met with school site leaders was to begin to offer the services of my department to assist in exploring and creating maker-based activities. I shared videos, research, make ready EDU resources, and offered to do PD with departments and school sites that were interested. One such elementary school took me up on the offer, and we hosted the district's first-ever parent Saturday maker event. It occurred in the fall of 2015 and had two components. Families rotated through a lab and were introduced to MinecraftEDU with server masters that were students in elementary and middle school. Parents had an opportunity to ask the questions about the Minecraft platform, why their kids watched so many YouTube's of Minecrafters and spent so many hours building Minecraft worlds.

In the multipurpose room, we offered three maker stations that were no tech - low tech. Families got a chance to build together, play together, problem-solve together, in ways they had never done at a school site event. The Principal shared that it was the first event that had ever been heavily attended by dads.

What followed was an introduction to the whole staff shortly thereafter, and the creation of a makerspace check out room with kits that kids could take home and tinker on their own. Not all teachers at the school have embraced the maker mindset, but I believe that small changes make big impacts as I have seen great examples of a large number of teachers at that school infusing the maker mindset spirit into instruction.

The next school year, we begin laying the framework for more professional development led by students and the Technology Services team covering concepts of infused in the maker model, like green screen, coding, and robotics. One of our two middle schools created actual maker courses as part of the wheel of electives. The budget was created, and the teacher was able to select low-tech no tech and some high-tech elements of the curriculum that would be delivered throughout the year. The school is now in the second year of delivering maker classes as part of the elective wheel for all grade levels. The hope is in the next school year, to begin cross-curricular exploration with the maker teacher working side-by-side with all other departments creating projects that are both real-world based and meaningful for the students. On that topic, *I will have to keep you posted.*

This school year, another school has created a maker exploration space as an Integral part of the campus. The space will have primarily no tech low tech options but as the space is better utilized by parents, students, and teachers, we will see if there are needs that dictate purchasing and implementing high tech solutions. The teacher that led this effort attended some of the training offered in green screen, coding, Makey

Makey, and video production. In summer school, she built her lessons around this mindset and shared examples of student work that looked like what you would see at a MakerFaire event.

We are a one high school district, and the school site also has begun this year with exploring the maker movement as an element of Future Ready Librarians. We are in the early stages of creating maker-based activities for a very large school site in meaningful ways. My team in partnership with the staff in the library are discussing what options will work best at such a large campus. We will be facing challenges facing things like 3-D printers due to the sheer numbers alone of how many students we serve. We are thinking about offering maker-based activities wrapped around spirit themes throughout the school year as our first effort. *This is another area I will have to keep you posted on as it is too early to share any successes or failures.*

Shifting culture is no easy business, but due to the very hands-on nature of the maker movement, I will say it is totally possible in short order if you are clear on the systemic vision and goals you hope to achieve. I don't want to see makerspaces at every school. I want to see maker-based education often occurring in every applicable classroom. Best of luck as you begin this journey.

About the Author

17+ years as an Educational Technology Administrator/Teacher. Moving organizations to the forefront of technology integration will better prepare our students for the new workplace. Differentiating the instruction by introducing coding design, problem-solving via gameplay (i.e. Minecraft), and collaboration online with cloud tools are all invaluable for hooking kids. I am an advocate for BYOD/T in schools. I want to help bridge poverty gaps by exposing students to technology. Information access to knowledge is the way.

MAKER PD: ACTIVE PROFESSIONAL LEARNING THAT SPARKS CREATIVITY

By Jacie Maslyk

It's a chilly February day as teachers trudge into the high school auditorium for yet another day of in-service training. They are less than enthusiastic as they find a seat and hunker down for a lecture-style session that is of little interest to them. They've brought papers to check. Some plan to read the newspaper. Others will occupy themselves by trolling Facebook or playing games on their phones. Sadly, this professional development example probably sounds familiar to many educators.

What if, instead of following this dull script, the teachers were challenged with a literacy-themed scavenger hunt including engineering design challenges?

What if teachers weren't confined to the auditorium but instead were divided into teams and provided with opportunities to collaborate, build, explore, and get creative?

What if teachers were encouraged to think across disciplines and work together in a hands-on way?

My district is in a professional learning transition, as we shift our practices away from traditional professional development to a more hands-on approach that includes *Maker PD*. It started a few weeks before *Read Across America* week. Our leadership team planned an unconventional day of learning that allowed us to focus on our goals of student engagement and increasing reading achievement, while also encouraging our teachers to work together. They built towers with red SOLO cups and white paper (think *The Cat in the Hat*), building for height and strength. Teams scrambled all over the building to answer scavenger hunt clues. They recreated famous book covers using video and green screen technology. They also enjoyed a photo booth complete with Dr. Seuss-themed props. This approach took teachers out of their comfort zones and pushed them to think flexibly and creatively about their own learning. It was the first time we ever tried anything different—it was a turning point for our professional learning vision that included a strand of making as a pathway to new learning.

Ok, so what does *making* mean? My definition of making is:

> An opportunity to learn through hands-on/minds-on work that fosters curiosity, creativity, and innovation through messing, building, designing, hacking, and remaking.

Making is now an established feature of many schools. In turn, school teams are finding the need to design experiences to support this new type of learning for educators. Hands-on making can occur within professional learning of all kinds, similar to the way it was embedded into language arts content in the opening story. Maker PD can also be explicit instruction in making techniques and skills such as learning how to solder or create something with a 3D printer.

Many schools are embracing the Maker Movement and including dedicated learning spaces within their schools. Making can happen in libraries, digital fabrication labs, STEAM studios, and inside every classroom. This chapter will provide some insight into professional learning that supports hands-on making, including stories from school leaders and educators who are implementing this type of professional learning in their schools.

Shift in learning

We are embarking on a new chapter in my school district with new leadership, new ideas, and a new focus. As we prepare our students for the future and promote the acquisition of the 4 Cs (creativity, collaboration, communication, and critical thinking), we must also build these 21st-century skills within our teachers. Gone are the days of the "sit and get." We can't sacrifice time with our teachers by disengaging them in passive learning experiences! Instead, we must be intentional about planning relevant learning opportunities that meet district learning goals and teacher interests.

In my district, we re-evaluated our professional development plan to ensure that it infused content, lots of team building, and a little fun. We hope that as teachers begin to look differently at their own learning, they will also reconsider the learning opportunities that they provide each day to our students.

With a desire to see more engagement in our classrooms, our district began to include STEAM, Making, and project-based learning into our K-12 instruction. In turn, we set out with a goal to transform our professional learning with the 3 E's in mind:

- Encourage
- Equip
- Engage

These three ideas guided our work to ensure that we were providing meaningful learning opportunities but also practicing what we were preaching. If hands-on learning is important in our classrooms, then our professional development needs to reflect hands-on learning. If we believe that technology is engaging and relevant to our students, then we need to provide teachers with quality experiences using new tools in meaningful ways.

Encourage

In many schools, PD is passive and has been for a long time. Making as a practice is social and collaborative. It does not fit into lecture mode. If you are used to sitting in a large auditorium and simply listening, then collaboration may feel uncomfortable for you. In turn, you may not encourage collaboration in your classroom. Encouraging teacher collaboration and active engagement in learning are critical to the mission of schools. When it comes to maker learning, collaboration is an essential component of effective professional learning.

As my school district embarked on a new vision for professional learning, encouraging teachers to connect with one another through making helped to build a Maker Mindset. This shift in thinking is at the core of Maker PD. Building capacity for teachers to use making in their classroom requires time and space for learning. To develop a Maker Mindset, learners need time to tinker, practice, connect, and reflect. Encouraging this mindset and exposing teachers to learning in this way is a work in progress. There isn't one "right" way to make. Each school must create their own path that supports their purpose.

Tinker

Tinkering as a strategy for learning may include messing around with new materials, figuring out how things work, and manipulating materials in new ways. Tinkering is accessible to everyone. *Here's some stuff. What can you do with it? How might it impact learning in your space?*

We carved out time within our professional development plan to allow time for teachers to tinker with new materials. A new game, a variety of materials, or the latest tech tool; tinkering with things in an informal setting was one pathway to further learning for some teachers. The casual nature of tinkering opened their minds to potential instructional changes and opportunities to infuse tinkering into their classrooms. Exploring with "tinker trays" or messing with circuits to light up an LED, learners have the chance to try out new things. Consider the ways that tinker can be used in your school or organization to develop maker learning.

Practice

Tinkering is a natural entry point for many learners. Low stakes. No pressure. Just try it. But it is vital to provide more structured time to practice new maker skills. We made sure to embed time within our professional learning for teachers to practice new skills like sewing, coding, or sculpture.

MAKERS IN SCHOOLS:
ENTERING THE FOURTH INDUSTRIAL REVOLUTION

At a recent tech-centered learning day, teachers self-selected multiple learning sessions throughout the day with open blocks of time for teachers to practice what they learned. Attend a session on using Canva (a cool graphic design software) and then jump right into the next session? No! Our teachers had an additional chunk of time to try out the software with support from the presenter as well as colleagues. Time to practice with LED wearables helped our teachers to improve their skills and think about ways to embed this new learning into their classroom instruction.

Think about it — we go to conferences or workshops and get great ideas. Maybe we put them in a notebook or talk about it with a colleague, but do we devote time to figuring it out, pursuing that knowledge or practicing something new? Or does it get forgotten somewhere in the bottom of our bag?

Carving out time to practice any skill is the only way to get better. In Malcolm Gladwell's *Outliers*, he says that you need 10,000 hours of "deliberate practice" to become world-class in any field. If we want to be skilled maker educators, then time is a critical component of our professional growth.

Connect

Traditionally, education can be an isolating profession. You're hired and given your classroom. You get your students, close the door, and start teaching. Many teachers have functioned in this model for many years. While making can exist in isolation (I picture my grandmother sitting in her sewing room for hours with no interaction with anyone before emerging with a beautifully designed dress or skirt), but inside the school makerspace, there's often a collaborative buzz.

I recently walked into our junior high space and found small groups of students building with cardboard. Some were moving around the room looking for materials. Others were planning at their table. Another pair of students were talking with the teacher about whether they should use hot glue or Elmer's to get their cardboard to stick. It was a productive busy-ness. Learners were talking, planning, creating, disagreeing, wondering.

Conversations in a makerspace can lead to exciting discoveries and new ideas. Conversations can guide learners (both young and not so young) to pursue new passions. Connections are key to learning. How do you promote connected professional learning for educators?

Reflect

Making can be challenging, rewarding, and curiosity-building. You (and your students) are learning new things in Maker Education. This can result in feelings of anticipation, joy, and frustration, at times. It is important to take time to reflect on new learning. Maker journals are a great way to reflect. Creating the actual journal can be a fun project - all you need is some cardboard for the cover and a variety of pages in between for writing, sketching, or planning new projects.

Some teachers aren't comfortable reflecting on their practices. Including lots of options will support all types of learners. Reflection can also happen through blogging about your maker journey or connecting with other maker educators through social media. Twitter can be a positive reflection tool, as teachers post maker projects and new learning with others in the making community. Use hashtags

MAKERS IN SCHOOLS:
ENTERING THE FOURTH INDUSTRIAL REVOLUTION

#MakerEd, #Makerspaces, or #MakerPD to chat more about this chapter!

Developing Dispositions

During another professional learning day in my district, we focused our attention to reflect on learning about the dispositions that we want to instill in our students. Teachers acknowledged how important these are, but struggled to identify areas where they included these in their classroom practices. These dispositions (also referred similarly to the Habits of Mind) are the characteristics we want our students to develop so that they are successful in school, career, and in life. These dispositions are also fostered within maker learning.

Engineering Design Challenges are a great way to develop these dispositions, both with students and teachers. Infusing these types of tasks within professional development sessions can be one way to engage teachers in collaborative work while also getting their creative juices flowing. We tried the spaghetti and marshmallow challenge (building the tallest tower with limited materials and limited time) during one of our PD days last year, and it was amazing to see teachers trying something new. Just like our students, some took a leadership role and others mapped out a plan, while others sat back and observed. I watched them as they came up with elaborate design plans and built structures that failed fast. Some teams regrouped and created various iterations, while others stuck to their original plan and never veered off course.

The challenge enabled them to think critically about a problem, consider multiple perspectives, and tackle a challenge together, many of the same things we want our students to do. When teachers are learners, they find value in the experiences that help them to grow.

If teachers are going to provide maker learning experiences for their students, then they need to engage in the process themselves. Sometimes this includes what Ian Leslie calls "productive frustration." It is the process of learning where you encounter challenges but yet persevere and work towards a successful conclusion.

It was with this new direction that we also began to infuse the ideas within the Maker Movement into our professional development. The mindset of a maker is very different from the mindset of a traditional educator, so the professional learning needs to be different as well.

Early in the school year, we started planning some opportunities for teachers to think differently about their own learning. We infused engineering design challenges that required teachers to use the 4 Cs. We presented activities and problems that required out-of-the-box thinking. Within the learning, teachers developed dispositions like resourcefulness, thinking flexibly, and taking responsible risks.

Creating connections

Breaking down the silos and connecting with educators is a considerable part of maker professional learning. Connecting may mean having a conversation across a table with another maker. It may mean joining a session that another teacher is leading. It may also mean connecting virtually through online professional development or using social media like Twitter, Facebook, or Voxer. This connection was critical for a group of our teachers who were embarking on a new professional learning experience. As a part of the Beaver County Innovation and Learning Consortium (BCILC), teachers from three school districts joined together for shared professional development. The focus of the consortium is fostering creativity and innovative practices in schools. The work of the BCILC also includes the establishment of a makerspace in each member district. In turn, district leadership needed to prepare teachers for this new learning. With a multi-prong approach, consortium leaders created a pathway for hands-on teacher leaders to engage in skill building and also provided academic growth through a book study.

The logistics of bringing together people from three different districts during the school year is a challenge, so the team explored other ways to keep the teachers connected. While I wasn't an expert Voxer user, I had participated in a group over the course of the previous six months with a group of educator bloggers called the Compelled Tribe. Personally, I found support and motivation from this group and loved the idea that people from across the country could push one another's thinking in new and different ways. So, I brought this idea to our BCILC group.

We chose to read Innovator's Mindset by George Couros as a tool to get our educators thinking about what it means to be innovative. Each week we read a chapter or two and then hopped on Voxer to discuss the information. Questions were posted (see insert) to focus our weekly discussions. The book study allowed our group to stay connected and explore the dispositions that support innovation and maker education.

Equip

Expanding teacher knowledge and equipping them with the essential skills to lead maker learning in their space takes time and planning. Some teachers don't naturally think of themselves as makers, so providing time to tinker and practice valuable maker skills is an important component of Maker PD.

One of the best professional learning opportunities that I ever had was as the principal of an elementary school. Blessed to be in Pittsburgh, a maker-centered city, educators are surrounded by universities, museums, and theaters—so many opportunities to learn and grow. Each summer the **MAKESHOP** at the Children's Museum of Pittsburgh offers a "boot camp." It is essentially a crash course in making, exposing participants to a variety of skills, tools, materials, and experiences. In their second summer offering a free week of PD, I took a team of teachers, and we learned that making is tough. Teachers grappled with the open-ended nature of the tasks. They struggled with thinking about meaningful ways to connect making to their classroom content.

By the end of the week, they had these powerful reflections:

- "Making puts you in the position of being a learner which can be frustrating, exhilarating and every emotion in between."
- "Thinking outside the box for adults is not always in our nature."

- "Being presented with open-ended challenges with "no correct answer" is out of my comfort zone."
- "I never thought I'd be able to do that, but now I can't wait to share it with my students!"

We pack a lot of learning within each school day, for our students and our teachers. Extending that learning beyond the school day is one strategy that we used in my former school district. We held a series of after-school workshops where teachers could attend to build their skills in STEAM and Making. It was optional for teachers, and anyone was free to participate. Each week, a handful of teachers would stay and tinker with tools and work to prepare ideas for their upcoming lessons. For one particular session, our physical education teacher joined in. From his perspective, if the students were going to be soldering, then he better learn too!

These learning sessions were a way for teachers to explore maker learning in a way that allowed them to tinker, practice, connect, and reflect, but expanding teacher knowledge in the area of making is tricky because there are so many entry points. Some teachers come with very little content knowledge, while others embracing our DIY culture have skills in woodworking, cooking, or crafting. Open learning sessions can take the pressure off and invite teachers into the making.

Students as experts

Your buildings are filled with students, possessing young minds filled with creativity, who are probably more tech-savvy than you or I will ever be. Yet, we don't call on the expertise of our young people often enough, for fear that we will no longer be seen as the experts in the room. When it comes to making, many districts are empowering their students to take the lead and provide professional learning for their teachers.

Two years ago, as an assistant superintendent, I hosted a lunch group with some junior high students each week. We had opened a new makerspace in the building, and we wanted to build the capacity for student leadership. So, a group of about 20 students and I would meet and tinker with stuff. The students then planned our STEAM Walk (a foundation-supported event held in all middle-level schools in our county) which focused on STEAM careers and hands-on learning experiences.

The STEAM event was so well-received that we asked our students to lead a half-day of professional learning for our teachers. Students showed teachers how to program Spheros and modeled how Squishy Circuits could be used as a learning tool. They shared the many ways that Makey-Makey could be used in the classroom. They created marble runs in the makerspace with their teachers using clean recyclables and tinkered with Legos and K'Nex. This shared learning empowered the students to become leaders of learning and teachers to change roles and become learners.

Last year, our students had another opportunity to shift roles as leaders in the classroom. Our region hosts an incredible event called Remake Learning Days. It is a two-week showcase of the creativity and innovation in our schools, after-school programs, non-profit organizations, and universities supported by the Remake Learning Network. As a part of this celebration, our district hosted an event at each level-elementary, middle, and high with the students leading the charge. Our 3rd-grade students served as ambassadors welcoming visitors into our new makerspace. They shared their knowledge with teachers and community members around teach Osmo, Ozobots, and virtual reality in the classroom. Students showed teachers the power of learning simply by trying things out. This empowered our students and engaged our teachers. How might you tap into the potential of your students to provide Maker PD to educators in your school?

Engage

Maker PD is not the traditional sit-and-get. It is an active learning process that includes hands-on exploration and often new experiences. It requires engagement. It taps into the curious creature we all have deep inside. When asked about why the Maker Movement is so important, Gary Stager, author of *Invent to Learn* said, it fuels our "basic human impulse to create." How do you fulfill your impulse to create? Designing, remodeling, sketching, hacking?

Hacking as making

Tell any group of students that they will be ripping, breaking, and hacking things as a learning opportunity, and chances are you'll get their attention. Deconstructing things is valuable maker learning. As learners break things apart, they are able to analyze what's inside, how things work, and how to reconstruct them to do something different. Do your students get the opportunity to tinker in this way? Do your teachers? This can be one pathway in your Maker PD.

I spent ten years as an elementary principal and always wanted to keep professional learning engaging for my teachers. One area where it was often a struggle to keep things fresh was during faculty meetings. As a way to infuse maker education into our practice, we spent one faculty meeting doing some hacking. I gathered a bunch of board games from home and picked up a few others at some local yard sales (these are great places to pick up maker items, especially since board games might have missing pieces or parts that others won't want to buy).

Teachers were challenged to work in teams, with each team including one primary teacher K-3, one intermediate teacher 4-6, one special education teacher, and one special subject teacher (art, music, library, and physical education). The teams could use anything from any game, but their materials had to come from at least three different games. Teachers chose cards, game boards, dice, spinners, and figures from a multitude of board games. Each team then had to write the rules to their game. How many players can play? Who starts? How do you win? Are there any obstacles involved?

At the end of 30 minutes, the teams presented the games to the other groups. Some incorporated chants, challenges, and rewards for game players. As the teams presented their hacked games, they were smiling and congratulating one another for their innovative ideas. The opportunity promoted teamwork and creativity, both things that we were also fostering in our classrooms. The best outcome of this learning opportunity was that the teachers (unprompted) went back to their classrooms and tried something similar with their students. Some created "getting to know you" games with icebreaker questions for the beginning of the school year. Others incorporated math facts, vocabulary words, and science concepts to make the games more academic.

While we often think that making requires that we build something out of nothing, making can also mean hacking, repurposing, and reinventing as a part of creating and innovating.

<u>Tools to support maker learning</u>

There are a lot of learning tools out there that can be used to facilitate maker learning with teachers (and with students). One tool that I came across last year was the Extraordinaires Design Studio. While it is marketed as a "game," it is a tool that facilitates design thinking, creativity, and making. We used it during a professional learning day as a way to get teachers thinking and working together.

Extraordinaires has different cards that players or teams need to select. The first card is a character card. The options are out of the ordinary: an evil genius, a woodland fairy, a magical robot. Each done in a beautiful illustration, the characters are critical to the design process in the game.

Next, teams choose a project card. These cards provide the details about what needs to be designed for this character: a place to sit, a secret hideout, a device to carry something.

The last card selected is a hint card. These are meant to provide some support, tips, and a focus for the design task.

We broke the group up into teams of 5-6 teachers. Remember, these are a mix of K-12 educators of all ages, levels of experience, and content specialty. We were intentional about the groups, planning so that each team had at least one person who was tech-savvy, another who was artistic, someone with leadership capacity, and one naysayer.

The groups chose their cards, and they were off to discuss their task. Many groups were hesitant, not sure what to do, how to get started, or what the actual expectation was. Just like our students! We were intentional about the open-ended nature of the learning experience. Open-ended maker tasks push the thinking of those involved, promote dialogue, and build internal capacity. This task was uncomfortable for some groups, but the results were outstanding.

One group wrote a song and performed it for the large group—after designing a device to carry supplies for a soldier. Another group built a 3D model of a home for a mermaid. Another group designed and sewed a satchel, meant to be a "water carrier" for a woodland fairy. Every group **made** something: a costume, a drawing, a poem, a skit. They designed with empathy as they planned with the unique needs of each character in mind. This act of making combined with the collaboration required to complete the task resulted in professional learning that developed design thinking with our teachers that carried over in their classrooms—the ultimate goal of professional learning.

Plan for engagement

Finding ways to infuse making into professional learning may be a part of what you already do, but for our district, this was a new venture. So, for all the different schools, districts, and other educational organizations out there, take a minute to reflect on your professional learning plan. How does it encourage teachers to pursue new learning? Does it equip them with essential skills for innovative teaching and learning? Do teachers connect with others and engage in hands-on creation? Is it filled with mandated topics and traditional formats or does it offer personalization, collaboration, and fun?

Use this PD checklist to reflect on professional learning in your school, district, or organization include the following:

- Collaboration
- Thinking
- Active engagement
- Time to tinker
- Movement
- Dialogue
- Hands-on activities
- Guided practice
- Choice
- Laughter
- Reflection

<u>Networks of learning</u>

When you are learning something new, do you like to do so in isolation, or do you enjoy the support of others? With the growth of professional learning networks (PLNs) and an increased interest in collaboration, more and more networks of learning are sprouting in the educational landscape. Learning networks can be virtual or face-to-face. Social media tools like Facebook and Twitter have groups where like-minded learners can gather and explore ideas. While these types of connection help to build professional knowledge and collaboration, face-to-face networks advance maker learning by adding the social aspect of making. Maker networks like this exist around many major cities including Chicago, San Francisco, and Pittsburgh.

Remake Learning

The Remake Learning Network, established over 10 years ago, is an open group of innovators in the Pittsburgh region. Remake's purpose is to initiate new ideas and share best practices and new ideas through collaboration. They host regional events, promote in school and out of school learning opportunities, as well as "meet-ups" around the city. The meet-ups include early childhood education and maker learning. There are also working groups discussing social equity, computer science education, and STEM ecosystems. The network provides countless opportunities for educators to connect with innovative teaching and learning.

Beaver County Innovation and Learning Consortium

In my county, we are working to replicate the Remake Learning model on a smaller scale. Through grant funding, three districts, supported by our local intermediate unit, created a network of innovative educators and school leaders who are focusing attention on promoting the 4 Cs through STEAM and Maker Education. Our consortium has developed shared professional learning opportunities connecting educators across buildings and districts. We are taking teachers out of the classroom to visit local makerspaces and consider the innovative practices and programs available to our students.

MAKERS IN SCHOOLS:
ENTERING THE FOURTH INDUSTRIAL REVOLUTION

Conclusion

Think back to the opening scene of this chapter with a large group of teachers seated in an auditorium. While there may be some learning happening in that setting, this passive nature is not engaging. It is not equipping our teachers with the skills and dispositions that they need to create innovative lessons that develop students as thinkers and innovators.

So, why are we still sitting in auditoriums???

Maker PD takes this into consideration and incorporates auditory, visual, verbal, kinesthetic, and tactile learning into the process. No PD is perfect but ask yourself - does it fuel your curiosity? Push your thinking? Make you consider new ideas?

How are you transforming professional learning to include Maker PD?

References

Couros, G. (2015). The innovator's mindset: Empower learning, unleash talent, and lead a culture of creativity. San Diego, CA: Dave Burgess Consulting.

Gladwell, M. (2013). Outliers: The story of success. New York: Back Bay Books, Little, Brown, and Company.

Martinez, S. L., & Stager, G. (2013). Invent to learn: Making, tinkering, and engineering in the classroom. Torrance (CA): Constructing Modern Knowledge Press.

Seuss, Dr. (1957). The cat in the hat. New York.

MAKERS IN SCHOOLS:
ENTERING THE FOURTH INDUSTRIAL REVOLUTION

About the Author

Passionate about teaching, learning, and leading, Jacie Maslyk, EdD has served in public education for over 20 years. An early implementer of STEAM and Making in schools, she currently serves as the Assistant Superintendent in the Hopewell Area School District and leads the movement for creativity and innovation in Beaver County with the establishment of the Innovation Learning Consortium. Jacie has worked in public education as a classroom teacher, reading specialist, elementary school principal, and Director of Elementary Education. A successful school leader, she was recognized as a National Distinguished Principal finalist in Pennsylvania in 2013 and 2014.

Dr. Maslyk has presented at the local, state, and national level on many topics, including educational leadership, STEAM, and the Maker Movement, and Innovation Literacy. She has done keynote speeches across the US and in Canada. She served as an Editorial Advisor for the National Association of Elementary School Principals (NAESP) Principal Magazine and has published a number of articles on Response to Intervention and Instruction, leadership, the Common Core, and instructional interventions. In 2015, she was awarded the Frank S. Manchester Award for Excellence in Journalism from the Pennsylvania Association of Elementary and Secondary School Principals (PAESSP). She is also the author of STEAMMakers; Fostering Creating and Innovation in the Elementary Classroom published by Corwin Press.

THE LEARNING LABORATORY

Michael Terborg

The library has been central to the community for centuries. The public library began as the "People's University" (Chancelor, 1938), a place to connect, learn new skills, and pick up new hobbies. The library has always been a place where people can learn, hear stories, and find reading materials that interest them. Today, it is this and more. It builds on these ideas and allows people access to tools they may not afford, may not realize they're interested in, or don't have a regular need for. Libraries now have tools, fishing poles, artwork, and more. (Soniak, 2015). It is a playground (Terborg, 2018); a place to play with ideas, constructs; creating stories that connect the digital and physical. It is a laboratory; a place to experiment. A library is a place where one has the freedom to follow one's own path while also coming alongside others to learn from them.

History

The educational community has long realized the child is the center of learning. While society has struggled with this as evidenced by large class sizes, scarce or expensive materials, and pedagogy, in the 1800s, Maria Montessori's teaching methods and Lev Vygotsky's Constructivism introduced us to more child-centered approaches. Both of their methods/theories focus on starting with what the child knows, giving them well-designed opportunities to explore, and opportunities to play and discover their world around them.

MAKERS IN SCHOOLS: ENTERING THE FOURTH INDUSTRIAL REVOLUTION

What does play have to do with learning? Everything. Just look at a young child. He or she is usually curious, exploring everything, assimilating new knowledge and building on it as he or she creates novel meanings. As a school librarian, I have noticed students have some difficulty with creativity. For example, one year I had my students design their own library cards. The only direction I gave them was to draw a school-appropriate picture. However, students repeatedly asked me what they could draw. A library is a place where students can research both what they're interested in, and what they need for class. This chapter will look at several strategies I believe can form a foundation of a learning laboratory; a place where students can experiment with information; connecting that to physical or digital forms.

The Fourth Industrial Revolution

The Library is positioned to play a key role here as we move into the fourth industrial revolution. Earlier technological revolutions brought us from steam power to the information age; the fourth will blend physical, biological and the digital realms (Schwab, 2016). The fourth industrial revolution is also about creativity. We will need creative individuals, teams, organizations, etc. to solve the technological and societal problems that will come from Artificial Intelligence (AI), robotics and other changing systems (environmental, geological, etc.). The library is a good place to serve as a creative laboratory. One can gather ideas from books, movies, and other sources to design simple prototypes that both resonate with children's imagination as well as integrate adults needs. This laboratory allows our young scientists, engineers, artists, and others to interact with materials in ways that may remind adults of a playground

(Behrs). That is, a place where children can play safely, in ways that are developmentally appropriate, yet with the freedom to explore, interact, examine, and create.

Here children can have ample opportunities to take their content knowledge, whether personal or academic, and create something by tinkering. Through tinkering, children can build a 3D or 2D model of their learning. Tinkering, which can be defined as *experimenting with materials and ideas to fully understand their capacities, and iterating to find better solutions to current problems* (Tinkerlab), is purposeful, succeeds at generating new ideas, and helps foster curiosity at a level appropriate to children's neurological and physiological development. While I have yet to use tinkering extensively with my students, I have allowed them to explore Scratch Jr. and numerous circuit boards that connect the physical to the digital.

Considerations for equity

As the makerspace is developed, it is essential that one keeps equity in mind. The library provides access to all social, ethnic, and economic classes to a variety of resources. The fourth industrial revolution is like earlier revolutions in that new technology can be expensive, difficult to learn, or present other access barriers. As such, the library can be a place where everyone can participate in exploring and learning about their world around them.

How does a makerspace help the English Language Learner? A makerspace allows children to demonstrate the full extent of their learning without having to rely on mastery of the English language. For example, students could pull out robots and learn how to use drag-and-drop blocks of code to program their bots; acting out stories in their minds (Language Magazine, 2017).

In 2012 Girls Who Code was founded by Reshma Saujani when she realized girls in computer science classrooms were lacking (Saujani, 2017). Making certain programs are accessible to all is critical, and there are several ways of doing this. Starting in early childhood, boys and girls should experience technology, building, creating, etc. together. Learning together enables children to experience things they might not be exposed to, learn about their strengths and interests as well as those of their classmates, and come to an understanding that boys and girls can have similar or different capabilities and interests.

This is especially relevant as we need to teach our young men and boys how to respect young women and girls in this space; treating each other as equals while they learn from one another. Also, it helps students learn to communicate with their peers. It is important to keep in mind that while women fill close to half of the jobs in the US economy, make up over half of college graduates, they only hold one-quarter of STEM-related positions (Sheffield, 2017).

Makerspaces in school libraries

A Makerspace approach to integrated STEM education is the deliberate positioning of student learning in contexts that require the drawing together of skills and knowledge from the areas of science, technology, and mathematics to create, construct and critique a product that has one or more engineering design elements. Products are usually selected by the participant and are often unique in nature (Sheffield, 2016).

What does this look like in a school library? The makerspace you develop will vary depending on the needs of the community and its resources. Typically, you'll find a blend of high tech and low-tech materials (Hlubinka, 2013). One can start with cardboard, duct tape, art supplies, and other up-cycled materials (Schreiber, 2016). No matter where one decides to start, it is important that one keeps in mind the interests, skills, and abilities of your teachers and students.

One way of designing makerspaces is creating activities around simple and complex machinery. In many districts, students are introduced to simple machinery in early elementary. Giving students the opportunity to work with these tools will give them an understanding of basic physics before one starts adding electronics. Students can then start adding circuits to start developing complex machinery or LEDs, sound, or other electronics. One example of this is having students build a paper city, add LEDs, and then write a story to narrate an experience in the city.

What results can one see from a makerspace? From personal experience at Tufts University's Early Childhood Development Center, I came to realize the power of the makerspace. Following the early childhood design process, children were introduced to a design activity. Here, students were to create their own room.

First children gathered ideas through the reading of a story then they generated ideas for their room, and then they created their room. Initially, this group of second graders was working in a way like co-play. That is, children had their own individual ideas and were trying to develop them independently of one another until they discovered they were running out of materials. At this point, they were prompted to work together.

Once children started working together, the communication blossomed. They began working in a cohesive team. Everything became better. The children demonstrated various social-emotional skills: collaboration, turn-taking, respect for ideas, property, willingness to work together, and more.

Children also used their imagination to make their model. A ruler became a rock-climbing wall, chenille sticks became a trampoline, and so on. The session ended with a gallery walk where children explained their ideas to the other groups. This model could be replicated in other libraries.

Engineering Design Process

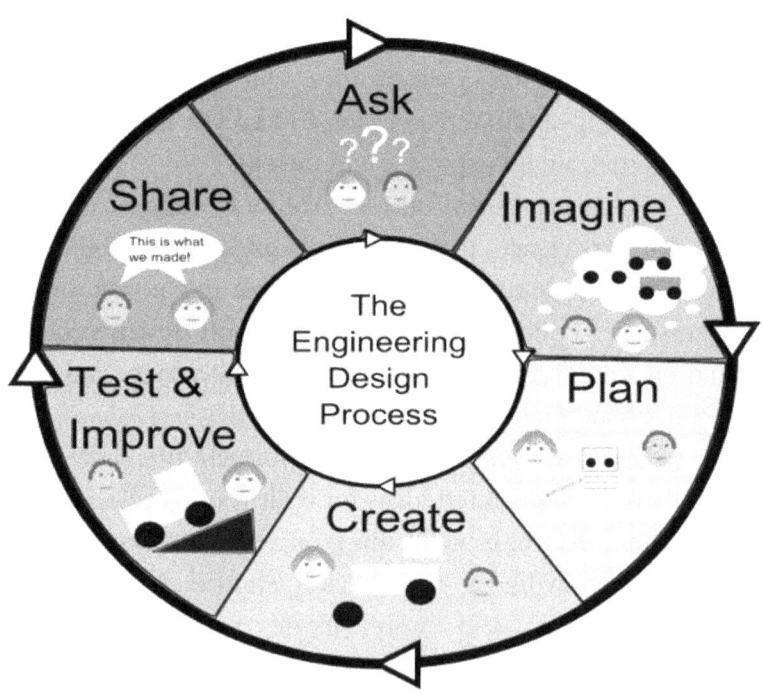

Created by The DevTech Research Group at Tufts University

This simplified version of the engineering design process was developed by the DevTech research group at Tufts University and is designed for use in the early childhood classroom. The process originates with the powerful idea, and then students are provided with the template in the diagram. This framework provides students with a structure to work through as they create (Bers, N.D.). A powerful Idea is one that focuses on central concept and skill, one that is personally useful, interconnected with other disciplines, and connects to prior knowledge (Bers, 2017).

From personal experience at Tufts University's Early Childhood Development Center, I came to realize the power of the makerspace. Following the early childhood design process, children were introduced to a design activity. Here, students were to create their own room.

First, children gathered ideas through the reading of a story then they generated ideas for their room, and then they created their room. Initially, this group of second graders was working in a way similar to co-play. That is, children had their own individual ideas and were trying to develop them independently of one another until they discovered they were running out of materials. At this point, they were prompted to work together.

Once children started working together, the communication blossomed. They began working in a cohesive team. Everything became better. The children demonstrated various social-emotional skills: collaboration, turn-taking, respect for ideas, property, willingness to work together, and more.

Children also used their imagination to make their model. A ruler became a rock-climbing wall, chenille sticks became a trampoline, and so on. The session ended with a gallery walk where children explained their ideas to the other groups. This model could be replicated in other libraries. For more information about the DevTech Research Group, please visit their website: http://sites.tufts.edu/devtech.

Another system is the Launch Cycle, and it focuses on design thinking (Spencer, 2016). It was developed by John Spencer and A.J. Juliani, it consists of 6 steps:

- L: Look, Listen, and Learn
- A: Ask Tons of Questions
- U: Understanding the Process or Problem
- N: Navigate Ideas
- C: Create a Prototype
- H: Highlight and Fix
- And finally, Launch to an Audience

As students move more into making or project-based learning, they will need new methods for documenting and organizing their research and process. Both of these frameworks are ideal starting points for project design.

Project ideas

What type of projects can students create in a library? Here are some ideas.

Storytelling

While many people think about makerspaces just for science, technology, engineering, and math instruction, it can also play a valuable part in literacy instruction. For example, when using the green screen, students can remix favorite fairy tales, imagine new endings for a book, create dialogue for characters, (Zubrzycki, 2016) Laura Fleming, a librarian in New Jersey who believes *"transmedia storytelling is the future for makerspaces. It is about how you can expand what you're doing with the kids across multimedia platforms. Instead of a one-and-done project, this is more of an **experience**."* Using wordless picture books, she has students look for ways to extend the story and look for ways to extend the story rather than making a digital representation of something found in the story; taking one deeper into the story (Fleming, 2018).

There are additional benefits to storytelling. According to Dr. Phil Zak, stories can be so engaging that they can cause one's brain to react as if one was a character in the movie. Good stories change brains possibly by increasing one's Oxytocin levels. In one research study, changes in oxytocin had a positive correlation with participants' feeling of empathy (Zak, 2015).

iMovie / Green screen

iMovie, a movie editing tool, can be used to help students tell their story, through the use of video editing. Another tool, green screens, can allow users to superimpose a background, further enhancing their creativity in storytelling. Here's how we have used it in our library.

First, we provided a simple introduction to iMovie. After showing students how to record, students were divided into pairs and asked to record each other reading their favorite stories. While they had difficulty balancing the cameras due to poor fine motor control, they were adept at recording and reading in front of the camera. A second cohort was introduced to the green screen. Children read fairy tales, illustrated their own backgrounds and characters, and then performed in front of the camera. Cameras can also be used for research. Children can research topics that relate to either their personal interest or to the curricula. Students can design their own visual aids, write their scripts, and then present their materials.

Playing with these tools allows for self-discovery; satisfying children's need for curiosity. It also enables them to build a foundation for future learning. With the popularity of many YouTubers as well as younger and younger podcasters, this is now a normal means of communication for even our youngest learners. Furthermore, children are now integrating language from their video games, podcasts, YouTube shows, and other electronic activities into their daily lives. They are also researching how to beat obstacle courses on YouTube and other online sources.

Finally, children go outside and talk about checkpoints, teleporting, and other concepts that relate to their online activities. This integration is a normal part of child development and identifying best practices and ethics is essential for establishing a foundation for adapting our educational system to meet the needs of the future.

Coding & robotics

I first developed an early elementary coding program in 2015. After introducing students to Scratch Jr., students were given the freedom to explore. I believe that children will discover what they're ready to learn or if they cannot they'll ask their peers. I believe that adult interaction should be minimal. However, if one does insert oneself, introduce it to one of the class outliers and then have him or her teach the others. After exploration, children can be given specific challenges such as creating a story, digitally animating a favorite book, designing a game, illustrating characters and backgrounds, and more. My students were still at the exploration stage; however, they learned a number of social-emotional skills. They learned to work together by showing each other various tools such as the camera, art pad, and microphone. They were excited when they were able to show their peers or teachers their projects.

Bridging coding and robotics, Scratch Jr. and KIBO robots provide an excellent foundation to build on. Both of these tools are designed for early elementary, are block-based, and are based on the ideas of Seymour Papert. KIBO also uses a physical block-based code system. Students do not use a screen to interact with the robot. KIBO, designed by Tufts University, is an expandable platform that students can add various parts to build complex systems.

Older students can also use Scratch, Apple Swift, Tickle App, and other popular coding tools. Other examples of good robots for elementary aged students include RoboWunderkind, also modular in nature. Edison, Lego, BeeBots, Dash and Dot, are other examples of good robots for elementary aged students.

There are many robots and other tools out there, and this document is not an attempt to reproduce that list. It simply highlights a few of the popular ones or ones that seem to meet Simon Papert's goal of Constructionism (Kafi, 2005). As you decide on tools, robots, and other equipment it is imperative that you keep in mind your community. What works for your students may or may not work for others.

Pocket computing, microcontrollers, and physical computing

Along a similar vein, as computers are getting smaller and smaller, there are several devices to watch. These include the Micro:Bit, Raspberry Pi, many microcontrollers such as the UK's Crumble, the LilyPad, Makey Makey, and more. All these can be used in physical computing. Physical computing is the integration of the computer and the physical world. This new medium is where the computer or microcontroller interacts with the physical world through various sensors, pads, and other input devices.

A learning laboratory or makerspace is a good place for students to tinker with all these tools. They can begin to manipulate their world with simple machinery, documenting their process, creating new products and sharing them with an audience and then as students become more adept at simple machinery, they can explore electronics, circuitry, and other tools.

There are a few different entry points into makerspaces: low - tech, using things previously used in arts and crafts, visual arts (green screen, iMovie, etc.), coding, robotics, physical computing, as well as hand tools, sewing machines, and other traditional tools. Makerspaces are more about philosophy than specific tools. However, as one designs a space, it is important to have tools and materials that are readily available to participants. They shouldn't need to ask for things. They should get what they need from spaces or storage that are within their reach. Tools should also be that would be appropriate for an adult but in a child-friendly size.

Circuitry

I introduced Makey Makey to a group of PreK students. A Makey Makey is a circuit board that allows one to use physical objects to control the computer. It was fascinating watching them figure it out. By holding hands, children were successful at making the computer create sound. Then one of the children broke the circuit. It took another child a few minutes to figure out why the music stopped and then he exclaimed: "Junior's not holding hands!"

Later I asked the students what would happen when I touched a container of water. A child looked at it for a minute and replied. "It will make music." He then stopped himself as if he realized water cannot make music. He was so excited when I touched the water and played music. Experiences like these are what stimulate children's minds and pique their curiosity.

Conclusion

What kind of citizens do we want our learners to become? This is a complex question, one that requires significant thought. One way to do this is through Positive Technological Development (*PTD)* which *"challenges us to design spaces by asking questions such as: What kind of learners do we want our young children to become? Curious innovators? Creative problem solvers? Critical thinkers? Caring collaborators? Active citizens?"* (Bers, 2012) Bers believes there are 6 C's to PTD Content creation, Creativity, Choices of conduct, Communication, Collaboration, and Community building.

As you design your makerspace, keep in mind that the physical design of the makerspace space conveys the type of learning one is promoting and what is most valuable in the educational process. In the makerspace, makers should be exploring digital competency, self-expression, and community formation through the creation of physical or digital products.

While this chapter may seem to focus on libraries, one should not limit the discussion to libraries or other large spaces. Larger tools like 3D printers, CNC machines, and other expensive things may be found in a space designed specifically as a makerspace, makerspaces should be found in every classroom. Start simple, possibly with center rotations, at a single table or station.

Resources

AASL's Best Websites for Teaching & Learning 2018. https://standards.aasl.org/project/bw18/

Curiosity Commons - https://curiositycommons.wordpress.com/makerspace-resources/

Dryden Elementary Art - https://drydenart.weebly.com/

How to Stock Your Makerspace for 100 Bucks or Less; Plus, an Essential Equipment List from the MakerBus Driver - https://www.edsurge.com/news/2016-05-24-how-to-stock-your-makerspace-for-100-bucks-or-less-plus-an-essential-equipment-list-from-the-makerbus-driver

Maker Educator Micro Credentials - http://makered.org/professional-development/maker-educator-micro-credentials/

Makerspace Resources, Renovated Learning - http://renovatedlearning.com/makerspace-resources/

Makerspace Resources and Programming ideas - https://colleengraves.org/makerspace-resources-and-programming-ideas/

Makey Makey - http://makeymakey.com

References

Aldama, Frederick. "The Science of Storytelling." *Projections*. 2015.

Bers, Marina Umaschi. Amanda Sullivan, Alana Strawhacker, *The Missing T & E in Early Childhood STEM: Young Children as Programmers and Engineers*.
N.D. https://successfulstemeducation.org/sites/default/files/Missing%20T%20and%20E%20in%20STEM.pdf

Bers, Marina Umaschi. "The Seymour test: Powerful ideas in early childhood education". *International Journal of Child-Computer Interaction*. 2017.

Bers, Marina Umaschi, Amanda Strawhacker, Miki Vizner, "The design of early childhood makerspaces to support positive technological development: Two case studies", *Library Hi Tech*. 2018. https://doi.org/10.1108/LHT-06-2017-0112

"Documenting and reflecting on making". *Bloomboard*. N.D.

Chancellor, John. "*The Public Library: A People's University*. Alvin Johnson," *The Library Quarterly* 8, no. 4 (Oct. 1938): 542-544.

Cunniffe, Aidan. "Creativity will be the source of our next industrial revolution, not machines". *TechCrunch*. 2016. https://techcrunch.com/2016/04/21/the-automation-revolution-and-the-rise-of-the-creative-economy/

Duckworth, Angela. *Grit, The power of passion and perseverance*. https://angeladuckworth.com/grit-book/

Fleming, Laura. "Makerspaces, a Passing Trend". *Worlds of Learning.* 2018. https://worlds-of-learning.com/2018/07/16/dont-let-makerspaces-be-a-passing-trend/

Gonzalez, Jennifer. "Are You a Curator or a Dumper?". *Cult of Pedagogy.* 2018. https://www.cultofpedagogy.com/curator-or-dumper/

Gonzalez, Jennifer. "To Boost Higher-Order Thinking, Try Curation". *Cult of Pedagogy.* 2017. https://www.cultofpedagogy.com/curation/.

Hlubinka, Michelle. "Stocking up School Makerspaces". *Make Magazine.* 2013. https://makezine.com/2013/08/21/stocking-up-school-makerspaces/

Kafi, Yasmin B. "Constructionism". Chapter 3. The Cambridge Handbook of the Learning Sciences (Cambridge Handbooks in Psychology). Cambridge: Cambridge University Press. Pp. 35 - 36.

Lewis, Dr. J. "Barriers to women's involvement in hackspaces and makerspaces".

Making Learning Come to Life. Language Magazine. Aug 2017. https://www.languagemagazine.com/2017/08/30/making-learning-come-life/

Nakamura, Jean and Mihaly Csikszentmihalyi. "Flow Theory and Research" *Oxford Handbook of Positive Psychology. Pp. 195 - 196.199.*

Nicholson, Simon. "*The Theory of Loose Parts: An Important Principle for Design Methodology.* https://ojs.lboro.ac.uk/SDEC/article/view/1204/1171

Paley, Vivian Gussin. *The Boy Who Would Be a Helicopter.* Harvard University Press.

Papert, S. "What's the big idea? Toward a pedagogy of idea power". *IBM Systems Journal*, v. 39, 3&4, 2000.

Schwab, Klaus., 'The Fourth Industrial Revolution: what it means, how to respond." *World Economic Forum."* 2016. https://www.weforum.org/agenda/2016/01/the-fourth-industrial-revolution-what-it-means-and-how-to-respond/

Shaffer, Leah. "Why 'Unlearning' Old Habits Is an Essential Step for Innovation". *Mindshift.* 2017. https://www.kqed.org/mindshift/48480/why-unlearning-old-habits-is-an-essential-step-for-innovation

Sheffield, Rachel et al., "Makerspace in STEM for girls: a physical space to develop twenty-first-century skills". *Educational Media International*, 54:2, 148-164, 2017.

Saujani, Reshma. "Girls Who Code Turns Five: What I've Learned Since Our Founding". *Medium.* 2017.

Schreiber, Mark. "Upcycling and the Low-Tech Makerspace". *Edutopia.* 2016. https://www.edutopia.org/blog/upcycling-low-tech-makerspace-mark-schreiber

Spencer, Josh. A.J. Juliani. *The Launch Cycle: Phases 1-6.* 2016. http://thelaunchcycle.com/

Soniak, M. "11 Things You Can Borrow from Libraries Besides Books" *Mentalfloss.* Feb 2015. http://mentalfloss.com/article/61514/11-things-you-can-borrow-libraries-besides-books

The University of Stavanger. "Better learning through handwriting." *ScienceDaily.* 24 Jan 2011. www.sciencedaily.com/releases/2011/01/110119095458.htm

Terborg, M. "The School Library as a Learning Playground." *ImagineEd.* Aug 2018. http://www.educationthatinspires.ca/2018/08/16/the-school-library-as-a-learning-playground/

Tinkerlab. What is Tinkering? https://tinkerlab.com/what-is-tinkering/

Zak, Paul J. "Why Inspiring Stories Make Us React: The Neuroscience of Narrative". *Cerebrum v.2015; Jan-Feb 2015.* https://www.ncbi.nlm.nih.gov/pmc/articles/PMC4445577/

Zubrzycki, Jackie. "'Maker Spaces' and Literacy Instruction: Playing with Story." *Edweek.* 2016. http://blogs.edweek.org/edweek/curriculum/2016/06/makerspaces_and_literacy_instr_1.html

About the Author

Michael Terborg is a Library Media Specialist. Currently, he is working in an elementary school serving almost 1,000 students who are primarily English Language Learners. Before coming to the schools, he spent a summer working in North Dakota for the National Park Service, he has also worked at the National Agricultural Library and The U.S. Environmental Protection Agency.

Section II: Makerspaces in Specific Settings

Section II looks at the specific settings and populations where our authors share their successes and FAIL-ures (First Attempt in Learning) as their engaged students experience discovery, communication, collaboration, critical thinking, and creativity.

- **"Making" it Happen** by Keri Hennessy-Wilson
- **Makerspace and English Language Learners** by Clara J. Alaniz
- **MAKE-ing the Most of the Curriculum** by Jennifer Bond
- **Converging STEAM Technologies** by Dr. Ella Marie
- **The Classroom or Library as a Makerspace** by Jackie Gerstein, Ed.D.

"MAKING" IT HAPPEN: TRYING TO MOVE A STEAM/MAKER AFTERSCHOOL PROGRAM INTO DAILY INTEGRATION

Keri Hennessy-Wilson

When it comes to creating a STEAM and Making in your school, there isn't one book or site that you use to start these practices in your classroom, school or district. It's like a puzzle or Frankenstein's monster that you are piecing together to fit your students' needs. What works for one district may not work for another. This is my story of how I navigated through this world and my implementation from an after-school program into daily integration during the regular school day.

What started it?

Once upon a time, in a little city by the sea in Asbury Park, NJ, a principal and a technology coach put their heads together and created a program that was different from any other in the district. The trend was to have an after-school test prep program for a select population of students, the "bubble kids." But, who really wants to do work after school? Not the teachers and most definitely not the students. So, we wrote up a proposal to target specific skills and standards using STEAM activities. The STEAM Academy was born!

MAKERS IN SCHOOLS: ENTERING THE FOURTH INDUSTRIAL REVOLUTION

The first year

The first year was a year of trial and error. It is important to have the right people to work with, and a squad was assembled. We researched many STEAM initiatives, attended workshops to archive activities, combed Pinterest and the internet. We tried several ways to implement, but in the end, we decided to do theme-based planning. Themes were chosen, and groups were created. Some of the themes were Being Healthy, Holidays and All About Me. It ran for an hour Monday through Thursday and students rotated between 4 activities every two days.

The room was set up with recycled items like paper towel and toilet paper tubes, tons of water bottles and any junk that we could find from the supply closets that were no longer in use. An email was sent out to the staff asking for donations of recycled items, fabric, yarn, etc. We did also buy some Bee Bots, a Dash and Dot, and 3D printers. One of the lessons that we learned from this year was that you can NEVER have too much glue or types of paper.

Pros: Students were exposed to alternative, hands-on learning, and true collaborative growth work. They were taught how to work through struggle and rely on each other to find answers. There was also time for teachers to try things that they wouldn't ordinarily try. Failure was an option for the teachers and the students for the first time.

Cons: Teachers had to use way too much prep time for an hour after school program. The focus was too broad. We were in one big area split up, and it was extremely loud. It was also hard to pick up group projects or continue lessons because of absences and other activities.

The second year

Going into our second year, we learned from our mistakes from the year before and we hit the ground running. We changed the name from STEAM Academy to Innovation Lab. This could now be a space where "thinking outside the box" is applauded. The team also unanimously decided to survey the students and split into separate academies to work on interests. They were: STEAM, Makerspace, Robotics, Coding, and CSI/Forensics. Students rotated through these groups conducted a variety of activities and challenges.

This year's order consisted of a vat of glue and tons of arts and craft materials. It was important for the students to have their designs be functional, but also aesthetically pleasing. We added to our robot family with some Ozobots and Spheros. Scratch was introduced to transition from Code.org Hour of Code lessons. Students extended their coding knowledge base and were able to remix posted creations or make their own.

Pros: Groups were better managed. Students had a choice of what kinds of activities they wanted to do. Teachers managed their own lessons. Students who were shy and not typical high achievers had more success than they did in the regular classroom. Exploration of topics pushed them into building esteem and confidence. They became leaders in their own groups and were more willing to go back to the drawing board to do a redesign. They were also exposed to a variety of STEM fields through the different academies. We had five academies: Robotics, CSI, Coding, Makerspace, and STEAM. Each academy had students who excelled and was not always the stereotypical smart student. Many of our

Special Education students were leaders in areas like Engineering and Scratch.

Cons: You can't reach all students' interests. Materials can be an issue.

The third year

This year has taught me to be even more flexible. For our program to continue, we needed to go under the umbrella of the 21st-century grant. This meant different hours and staff. But, true to the Making spirit of starting over and redesigning, we are transforming once more. Relevance is a huge part of our focus and intentional instruction. Students were surveyed for what they love and hate about school, what worries them and their future aspirations. Again, we are building skills with our students that are essential for future projects.

Hip Hop Literacy was started for students to create graffiti art that reflected them. Students then took the word of the week from their classes and began working on art to demonstrate their comprehension. A future project will be to create a banner for the school. Through surveying, we found that there was a huge love of arts and crafts. I encouraged them to make these crafts and realized that there was a considerable problem with following directions. I literally had to walk students step by step through each project. They were not able to work independently, yet. A future project is to create their own videos to put on the district's YouTube channel. Stay tuned for more transformations...

Pushing STEAM & making into daily lessons

When I began as the Technology Coach in my building I was gung-ho and enthusiastic. This wasn't true for all of the teachers in my building. I had an open-door policy and invited teachers to sign up for help, and I always volunteered to come into the classroom to help. I had just a handful of teachers who would want help to incorporate technology, but usually, they just wanted me to fix their computers. I didn't give up. I went back to the drawing board. I went into classrooms, assisted when asked and provided training when asked. This wasn't enough for me, and it definitely wasn't enough for our kids in the districts. Plan A for integration of STEAM into daily lessons occurred during my training and coaching. I suggested the use of STEAM and provided examples using our anchor texts. Teachers were open to it, but there was no follow-through in their own classrooms. I attempted again (Plan B) to volunteer to come into classrooms to do model lessons and help in centers. Only a few teachers were interested. Enter Plan C...

I used the after-school program to try different STEAM/Maker activities and see how the students responded. The students were willing and open to anything that we did. If they didn't like an activity, they would definitely tell us. The biggest issue was pushing the students to work through frustration. We had to teach the students how to be self-sufficient and how to ask the right questions when they needed assistance. The staff also needed to learn how to be facilitators for support and not enablers. Students are used to teachers doing too much for them. Our after-school program worked through the STEAM design model and created stamina. We created this in a small part of our school population. Students who weren't traditionally known as "smart" were the ones who did the best with this idea. They were the ones who were flourishing. That was when the team had conversations about starting to move these activities into the day.

How do you move an after-school program into the day and have buy-in? It took me three years of tweaks and going back to the drawing board to come to realize I was doing the same thing the same way and expecting a different outcome. We all know what the definition of that is. I had to brainstorm on how I can reach teachers who have tech phobia or complacent in an intentional manner that can be rolled out easily. These are the steps I took to make this happen.

It was essential to me to meet the needs of our students in our district and get up to speed with the technology educational arena around us. I had to build capacity first. To begin my plan, I had to start adding to their tech toolkit < introducing various strategies and digital tools. Again, it goes back to not knowing what they don't know.

In my school, grades 3-5 are departmentalized, which makes it tricky to plan professional development and training. I first put together a technology framework with specific tools for K-2, 3-5 Math/Science and 3-5 ELA/SS. This would guide the learning in those cohorts, and everyone was introduced to Google Classroom to conduct their work collaboratively at any hour.

The Technology Framework is basically a checklist for me to keep my work intentional and focused throughout the year. It is a living document that is fluid and can be adjusted when needed. The framework was created with a STEAM/Maker mindset. The intention was to bring back more creativity in the classroom and move teachers away from a "teaching to the test" mantra that has plagued classrooms for years. But, just as we teach our students, we must set up a foundation and build scaffolds. The same must be done for adult students because of the varied levels of tech ability. The framework consists of guidelines, a timeline of implementation, and badges.

If you build it, they will come...sort of

We currently have one *STEAM lab,* and this year we have opened it up for teachers to bring their classes into it. These hands-on lessons that derive from the current curriculum. Teachers are encouraged to integrate subjects using standards as a base. This has been a little slow going with only a few teachers using the space. My big goal was to start archiving lessons to create a Digital STEAM/Maker Library for teachers to access.

Presently, my implementation of STEAM/Maker lessons is done during coaching sessions. Suggestions or next steps are provided as a resource that is STEAM-based. My reasoning for this is largely due to learning engagement. If your school is anything like mine, students definitely work better when activities are hands-on. We also must remember that we have to provide scaffolding to help them along with this process. Students can't be simply thrown into the design process and expect them to be successful. We are teaching with a spoon-fed generation of students, used to being given information and regurgitating it back on the test. To truly think on their own, with a little support, takes work and persistence. Two thumbs up for the movement and the roll-out of STEAM into classrooms.

Next, we are in the process of opening another "STEAM" lab. To help teachers take baby steps and I will be conducting lessons in the labs alongside teachers. I plan to use literature and specific grade-appropriate standards, to model lessons using STEAM ideals.

MAKERS IN SCHOOLS:
ENTERING THE FOURTH INDUSTRIAL REVOLUTION

This can be a daunting task. Where do you begin? For those who know me, you know that I LOVE Pinterest. It is my favorite way to unwind other than reading. It is one-stop shopping for ideas for anything in your life. But, when it comes to the work that I do, I am purposeful in the resources I choose. It is quick to simply choose from a board and run with it, but that is not enough for me. I choose something and use that resource to build a foundation or to spark another one. Next, I use my PLN (Professional Learning Network) for ideas. This could be from Twitter, Facebook, Instagram, Voxer, etc. I compile all the ideas in my PLN and remix them to fit my needs. Lastly, I am forming a partnership with Barnes & Noble. They have been a great resource for me. The Communication Manager sits with me to brainstorm ideas. She has direct access to other resources, professionals, tech equipment and books that can help me in the labs. Also, they make visits to our school to conduct STEAM activities with tools or equipment that we may not have. Our students are exposed to STEAM and Making in a variety of experiences.

In conclusion, trying to promote STEAM/Maker lessons at your school can be done. It's easy to get materials, but if you don't have the people to do it, it's not going to work. I've formed a squad, and we are spreading the word one teacher at a time. Each day as a coach is different. I can provide resources one day and co-teach the next. Making is not one size fits all. Don't buy equipment because everyone else is. My students weren't ready for certain tools because they lacked a complete foundation. Be prepared to stay the course, and in the end, your students will be exposed to a world of innovation; the future's world. If you build it, with supports, they will (eventually) come.

About the Author

Keri Hennessy-Wilson has been teaching for 18 years in New Jersey. She currently is a Technology Coach in Asbury Park, NJ. She is a wife and a mother to 3 daughters. Her hobbies are working out, reading and she is totally obsessed with Harry Potter.

MAKERSPACE AND ENGLISH LANGUAGE LEARNERS

Clara J. Alaniz

Imagine you are a student and have just been relocated to an area that speaks a language you do not understand. You don't understand their letters or other characters. You've been given some translation tools and know a few basic words, but you certainly are not fluent. The signs on the school walls advertising PTA meetings and after-school clubs make no sense to you. A teacher greets you with a warm smile, but her voice is in a different language and sounds like nothing you've ever heard in your life. You are in a classroom where the other kids are your age, but they don't speak English. You sit silently and wait for something, anything to make sense.

Later you are introduced to a group of kids who also speak English. You breathe a sigh of relief and ask them the many questions you were holding in. These kids quickly become your friends, and you rely on them to show you the ropes. You are often grouped with these kids, and you like that because your communication flows smoothly in English.

A year goes by, and you have learned more phrases in this new language and have a basic understanding of the letters/characters. It's easier to identify keywords and ask basic questions. Communicating is more natural and your skills are increasing. This is all very encouraging, but you know you have a long way to go before you can understand this new language in the same way you understand English. This early language acquisition is described by Jim Cummins as Basic Interpersonal Communicative Skills or **BICS**.

As time goes by, you rely on **BICS** to get you through many lessons as well as lunchtime, recess, and all other parts of your day. However, you still struggle. Today, a teacher is trying to teach you about improper fractions, and she is very warm and patient while working with you. But one part of your brain is translating all those new words into English as best you can while another part of your brain is learning how to convert improper fractions. Your brain is multitasking all day long because you must translate everything into English while you're also learning a concept. For a moment you think to yourself, "This would be much easier if I had a teacher who spoke English. I would learn this so much faster." But you remember there are only a few teachers at your school who speak English and the pressure to learn this new language is palpable.

It's hard to imagine that being your daily life, but that's how many English Language Learners feel every day. They are working toward Cognitive Academic Language Proficiency or **CALP**. Cummins describes CALP as the kinds of skills used in learning environments such as grammar and higher order thinking. According to Cummins, it can take seven years or more to develop academic language to the point that students can analyze information or evaluate evidence in a new language. After one year, a lot of growth in learning a language can occur, but it will be around six more years before reaching proficiency.

Children who are learning English are developing academic language (both **BICS** and **CALP**) every day while simultaneously learning concepts in mathematics, science, social studies, social skills, behaviors, and every other subject in school. Makerspace is one area that can help ELLs as they develop academic language, collaborate with others, build their confidence, and become future ready.

Failing forward

A valuable characteristic of Makerspace is being encouraged to make mistakes; we fall forward as we learn and create. The ability to view a mistake as a learning experience sounds easy, but we all know from experience that it can be hard. A mistake hurts because we are human, and we want to be successful. However, we need to fail because learning from mistakes is a skill that builds character and perseverance. Failing forward can also help us to utilize reflection as a way to make decisions and understand our own ways of thinking. We remember mistakes we made in the past and in new situations. We reflect upon that prior knowledge to help us make better decisions.

How adults react to the mistakes of students can affect how they internalize failure. In elementary school, I was laughed at by a teacher when I would say words in Spanish rather than English. Code-switching is when you alternate between languages, and it's a common occurrence when multiple languages are operating in your mind simultaneously. Even though code-switching is natural and not a mistake, I was made to feel ashamed of it. For years after that, making even the smallest mistake set off a sense of fear and humiliation in me. I was terrified of others laughing at me if I made any kind of mistake and the pressure to be perfect was a burden I carried into adulthood.

English Language Learners are often faced with the pressure to be perfect English speakers. They sometimes feel the need to learn the language as quickly as possible and can't make a mistake. They are sometimes told that natural occurrences, like code-switching, are mistakes. All of this negativity toward mistakes, real or perceived, can make students nervous and reluctant to participate in class. I often wonder what my high school and college years would have been like if I had learned to embrace mistakes as a young student. We can't change the past, but we can help kids, so they don't experience those kinds of issues.

Through makerspace, English Language Learners are given opportunities and are highly encouraged to make mistakes. They are supported when trying things multiple times and are praised for failing forward. They internalize the value of making any kind of mistake because those mistakes mean growth. They build confidence to try new things and thrive while learning in this way. All the beneficial characteristics of makerspace such as character building and perseverance will carry over to other aspects of their learning, including language acquisition.

Developing skills

One aspect of Makerspace with multiple benefits is taking notes. As learners work through their creations, they keep a log of what worked and what didn't work. Notetaking in Makerspace is a skill that promotes viewing any failed attempts in a positive light; they are taking steps toward a working solution rather than making a mistake.

With any camera tool or audio recorder, it's easy for students to communicate. Ask the students to do notetaking with an audio recording or a video in whatever language feels comfortable at first. As they become more proficient in a new language while also learning the concepts within their Makerspace project, they can slowly integrate the new language into their audio/video notes. Listening to/watching their notes will give them an opportunity to reflect upon their work on the Makerspace project and use that to help guide future decisions in other projects. It will also give them an opportunity to hear their own voice speaking in English while using academic language. This is an effective and fun way to develop their phonemic awareness and distinguish sounds in the English language.

Collaboration is a natural and engaging part of Makerspace. Try pairing kids who speak different languages together. Allow them the opportunity to teach each other and learn from one another. I understand the desire to partner kids who speak the same language so that the communication is smoother. But ELLs should develop relationships with their English-speaking classmates and have opportunities to communicate using academic language with native English speakers.

The academic language used within a Makerspace project will vary, but this method will give them a chance to practice without any pressure. Words such as troubleshoot, login, app, upload, download, video editing, fair use, feedback, screencast, and Creative Commons are just a few examples of academic language commonly used in Makerspace that boost digital literacy. Developing literacy is an obvious goal for ELLs, but they need digital literacy, too.

A study done in 2014 showed that 77% of jobs will require technology skills within a decade. We are now four years into that decade and look how much has changed in that short time. What will the workforce look like in four more years? Our students learning English need digital skills to be successful in the workplace, no matter where they choose to work. They need opportunities to be leaders and models of digital citizenship. Understanding how to make positive contributions in the digital world is a skill all users must have in the workplace and in their personal lives. Makerspace is a natural, creative, and interactive way to help develop those essential, lifelong skills.

ISTE Standards for Students

The ISTE Standards for Students were refreshed in 2016 and begin with Empowered Learner which encourage students to establish goals for themselves. The Knowledge Constructor, Innovative Designer, and Computational Thinker standards have obvious connections to makerspace such as making meaningful connections, refining prototypes, and breaking problems into component parts. I sometimes find that students learning English are not empowered to demonstrate their learning in different ways. Also, if those students are given an opportunity to establish their own goals, they typically relate to language acquisition only.

Their learning is targeted toward language acquisition, and the kids are often surprised when they get to do anything other than that. I've heard them say, "Are you sure I go, too?" when it's time to create in the Makerspace area. A truly empowered learner establishes goals and has input on how to reach those goals. Their goals should include digital skills, digital citizenship, language acquisition, and content area concepts. Learning a language or a concept doesn't necessarily have to be an isolated lesson; students can learn those things while also developing digital-age skills. ELLs are makers and should be encouraged and empowered to participate and learn in those areas.

ISTE Standards for Educators

The ISTE Standards for Educators were refreshed in 2017 and align with the ISTE Standards for Students. The standards are not a chart or a checklist; they are ways to be. They are aspirational goals for educators as they design learning experiences for students as well as develop their own digital skills. I was asked to serve on the Technical Working Group that refreshed the Educator Standards and what regularly came up in our meetings was equity, empathy, and empowerment.

The Educator Standards begin with the Learner Standard which encourages educators to continue their own learning. Allow your students to see you learning new things in new ways and failing forward. The Leader Standards promotes becoming advocates for equitable access. This could mean equitable access to online resources, but it also means equitable access to learning opportunities.

The Citizen, Collaborator, Designer, and Facilitator Standards discuss creating learning experiences which allow students to make positive contributions and collaborating with students to design those experiences. The Standards encourage educators to demonstrate cultural competency while designing innovative, student-centered learning environments and giving students the opportunity to take ownership in reaching their learning goals.

Empower the children learning English to establish a goal with a Makerspace project and support their steps toward reaching that goal. Encourage them to share their results, mistakes and all, so that they can make positive contributions and practice giving and receiving feedback.

MAKERS IN SCHOOLS:
ENTERING THE FOURTH INDUSTRIAL REVOLUTION

Advocacy

One question I regularly get is, "What makerspace projects are available for students learning English?" And my answer is, "Use the same makerspace projects as all the other kids." Many Makerspace projects do not require much speaking or writing. As mentioned earlier, pairing students with native English speakers can be very beneficial as well as allowing English Language Learners to take notes in a video or audio format in the language of their choosing. There will be some items that require translation, but that's true of anything they learn in school. Makerspace projects aren't any different because the children are learning English just as improper fractions are no different.

In some cases, English Language Learners are unfairly labeled as unintelligent or incapable. Just because a child is working to learn a language you have spoken all your life does not mean he or she is unintelligent. It means the child is learning in an entirely different way and demonstrating empathy and cultural competence, as suggested in the Collaborator Standard, would enhance the student's growth.

Two years ago, I saw a small group of kids who spoke different languages teach other English and Spanish while simultaneously working to get their robot to move in a specific direction. They encouraged each other, they supported each other, they believed in each other. Their collaborative spirit was enough to bring me to tears, and I only got even weepier when their robot moved. They jumped into the air and hugged. It was a moment in time that I never take for granted. It was a moment of growth that was being properly celebrated. I think of them daily and advocate for more of those moments because their learning is exactly why we do what we do.

Grow the cilantro

In 2017 at the ISTE Conference in San Antonio, TX, I gave an Ignite Speech about the ISTE Standards for Educators. I told the story about my parents' backyard garden which provides delicious produce for our family year after year. A few years ago, the cilantro that usually grows in the garden sprouted in the front yard. Then it sprouted by their outdoor grill. And later it sprouted all over their property. Rather than remove the beautiful blossoms, my parents allow the cilantro plants to grow anywhere they sprout.

That growth reminded me of what we do in classrooms every day. We see tremendous growth in the gardens that are our classrooms. We see unexpected growth. We see growth in areas some say we could not grow. Just like that cilantro, all our students have a right to blossom and grow anywhere they can. I encourage you to be that gardener who "grows that cilantro" and celebrates that growth. I encourage you to be that collaborative designer who creates student-centered learning experiences and give all our kids a chance, no matter what language they speak.

About the Author

Clara J. Alaniz is a 5th generation Texan and has been an instructional technology specialist for 17 years. She also served as an elementary school teacher. Clara is a certified principal and certified Technology/IT Director. She is the Advocacy Chair for the ISTE Administrator PLN and was selected to join the Technical Working Group that refreshed the ISTE Standards for Educators. Clara is a Google Certified Trainer and a Google Certified Educator, Level 1 and 2.

MAKE-ING THE MOST OF THE CURRICULUM

Jennifer Bond

My passion for creating

Throughout my career, I have always had a passion for creativity and making! I was fortunate enough to earn a minor in Integrated Creative Arts from Western Michigan University in 1998. In 1999, my first year teaching, centers were a large part of the curriculum, and it allowed me to think of creative ways to integrate curriculum and skills. I continued having centers and stations for many years. Some of my favorite centers were the Creation Station and the Take-Apart Station.

The Creation Station was essentially a bin full of upcycled materials and craft materials. Students could use the materials to create anything they would like to make, and then students would write about their creation. The Take-Apart station was inspired after my husband and I needed to replace our DVD player. I thought it would be cool for the kids to take it apart with screwdrivers and see what was inside. It was such a hit that I scoured my house for other outdated electronics and brought them in each week for groups to take apart. I eventually put out a call to my Team Bond families to bring in items too. I remember the excitement kids had when they found the circuit board and other pieces.

Years later I found out this was called Reverse Engineering. These types of stations were my early version of a classroom makerspace.

MAKERS IN SCHOOLS:
ENTERING THE FOURTH INDUSTRIAL REVOLUTION

I have also been heavily involved with Destination Imagination, which is a global, creative problem-solving program. Within DI, students are encouraged to be creative with materials and ideas to complete a challenge they have chosen, in addition to solving instant challenges that often involve making. Thinking out-of-the-box and combining materials in unique ways is the core of what makes Destination Imagination amazing. The program embodies the maker mindset and students from around the globe compete each year to showcase their innovation! If you would like to find out more about this awesome program, go to www.DestinationImagination.org.

Through my entire career making has been a part of my foundation, and I have tried to integrate it as much as I can to engage my students. In this chapter, I will highlight some of the ways I have brought maker experiences to life in my classroom.

Special times with making

Maker experiences don't have to necessarily be integrated each day into the classroom. You can give your students opportunities through special encounters. For example, Imagination.org sponsors the Global Cardboard Challenge and the Inventor's Challenge, which allows a bit of a structure, yet open creativity. The Global Cardboard Challenge was inspired by Caine's Arcade, a viral video created by Nirvan Mullick, that showcased Caine and his cardboard arcade games. The Global Cardboard Challenge takes place in early October and encourages kids to get creative with cardboard through play.

To participate in the Global Cardboard Challenge, all you really need is to register and then put out the call to your families to collect cardboard (perhaps 2-3 weeks before.) It also helps to let your custodian know to put some aside and find a place to store the collected cardboard. Next, have your class watch Caine's Arcade 1 and 2 to get inspired and perhaps share tips from the playbook, which will be available to you after registering. Cutting cardboard can be tricky, so you will want to think about that too. I typically keep a box-cutter in my pocket for adult use only. For little ones, Makedo (https://www.make.do) makes great cardboard saws that are safe. In addition, they have cardboard screws and drivers that make connecting the cardboard easy. If you can't get the screws, tape will be needed. Duct tape typically works the best. If you want to purchase duct tape for awesome prices (six rolls sometimes for $2), you can register for the **NAEIR.org Educator Program**, otherwise requesting donations from families works well too!

There are ways to connect it with the curriculum. For example, in the past few years, I have held the Pure Michigan Cardboard Challenge. Michigan geography is the unit of study for the fall, so I require the students to pick a geographical connection to honor for their cardboard creation. From recreating the Mackinac Bridge with cardboard to engineering a game themed around Comerica Park where the Detroit Tigers play, students enjoy using their creativity to bring elements of Pure Michigan to life. Literacy is also a great way to connect the cardboard challenge. Students could honor an author, a book, or a character with a cardboard creation. For a math connection, you could give students a list of requirements as far as integrating certain size pieces to practice measuring, particular shapes to integrate geometry, and even fractions. Otherwise, you can just let the kids be free with their creativity.

MAKERS IN SCHOOLS:
ENTERING THE FOURTH INDUSTRIAL REVOLUTION

In addition to the Global Cardboard Challenge, Imagination.org also sponsors the Inventor's Challenge. This typically takes place in the early winter and commences towards the end of February. Students are encouraged to think about a need or a problem they can solve with an invention. Like the Global Cardboard Challenge, once you register, you will be given a playbook with tips and ideas for your students.

Since 2011, I have been hosting an Innovation Day in my classroom. This typically occurs in late May and is a wonderful activity to have towards the end of the year. I first heard about it on Twitter from Pernille Ripp, after she heard about it from Josh Stumpenhorst, who had hosted one earlier that year. It is based on the 20% time that Daniel Pink refers to in his book Drive. Essentially, students have an entire day to decide what they are going to learn, what they are going to create, and how they are going to present something. Two-week ahead of time, I launch it and give time for the students to think of ideas and plan their day...including the steps they will go through and the materials they will need. The plan needs to be approved by both myself and their parents. I approve it by having a short conference with each student, as we discuss if they have enough to fill a day, if I need to provide materials, and give any suggestions that may be helpful.

A student wanted to make string art for his mom, who was raised in Alaska.

Once the day arrives, it is amazing to see how engaged and on-task the kids are for pretty much the whole day. There have been some amazing projects that have come out of Innovation Day over the years. What I love is the diversity of the projects. From composing original music to building a Lego boat to researching water diversion from the Great Lakes to duct tape purses, I have enjoyed seeing what happens when you turn over the reins to kids!

MAKERS IN SCHOOLS:
ENTERING THE FOURTH INDUSTRIAL REVOLUTION

After having many successful Innovation Days, I decided to increase the time of student-centered exploration, and I instituted Genius Hour in my classroom once a week. However, my students called it Goal Time at first. They would set a goal and work towards meeting that goal. Sometimes it was a one-week goal, while other times it was a multi-week goal. When I first started loom bracelets were the rage, so I saw a lot of looms at first, but then I showed them the connection to crocheting, which then led into knitting. Student businesses also were created during Goal Time including a very successful sugar scrub business, as well as paracord bracelet company. The businesses were a great way to connect our economy lessons that were required for social studies.

The following years, our Goal Time turned into Passion Time, and we have kept our once a week, one-hour tribute to focusing on passions. Students have found time to learn more about coding, sewing, circuitry, reading, drawing, Minecraft, playing instruments, engineering, and general creativity. It is one of my favorite times of the week, as there is such excitement over student-driven learning and exploring. I will also add that students are very gracious that I give them the one hour and think it is the very best thing ever! If you can find one hour each week, every 2 weeks, or even every month to give your students, I would highly recommend it!

MAKE-ing history come to life

Many teachers want to know how I have the time to do makerspace activities, as time is scarce with trying to fit in all the curriculum we have. Like the saying goes, "Kill two birds with one stone," integrating the making experiences with the curriculum is key. As I begin new units, I intentionally think of how I can fit making in, while teaching the standards.

I watched the documentary, Most Likely to Succeed. In the documentary, a Physics teacher and a History teacher team up to teach the rise and fall of ancient civilizations through gears. Groups of students had to create a system of gears to synthesize the rise and fall of an ancient civilization. As I watched, I thought to myself, what could I do that would help kids really think abstractly about something we were learning. At the time we were getting ready to learn about early explorers. I remembered seeing these cool paper roller coasters that one of my Imagination Chapter students brought to our meeting. It was then that I came up with the idea for the students to create a paper roller coaster that represented the life of their explorer...Early Explorer Roller Coasters!

When I launched the research report with the kids, I went over the normal research report criteria, as they had to write a report. I ended it by letting them know they would need to find out as much as they could, so they could design an awesome roller coaster themed around the life of their explorer. The excitement in their eyes could be seen, and I knew this was going to be a great project.

They were very eager to research and write their reports so they could get to the fun part of building the roller coaster. Once they were ready for the roller coaster design, I shared the requirements for the coaster...it had to have 5 purposeful elements that represented the life of their explorer. We used templates that I purchased from PaperRollerCoasters.com, which also came with an instruction manual that I printed for students to share. Each student received a cardboard base, and I had all of the elements printed on cardstock paper and organized in bins. Construction began with the columns and beams.

It was interesting to see the different ways students tackled the tasks. There was one group that chose to work together to create all of their columns and bases. Half of them scored the cardstock while the other half folded and taped. It was neat to see them team up together. It was also interesting to see the kids that rushed through it without following the directions on building the strongest structure. Most of the students had to start from scratch when their tower toppled. Throughout the process, I was able to integrate lessons on civil engineering and architecture, as well as measuring.

I heard over and over again, "This is hard!" I would reply, "Should we not do hard things? Would you rather not build a roller coaster? I can find some easy worksheets for you to do." The students would quickly say they were OK and would return to their coaster construction. It did take a lot longer than I was expecting, and yes, I did have to jump in and help students out. I even multi-tasked at night to build elements while watching TV, as some of the students didn't have the fine motor coordination to do some of the more complex loops and funnels. I had to constantly send out more requests for tape, and I continued to copy templates. Having 75 paper roller coasters also provided a storage issue, but luckily our school's stage wasn't being used, and we took it over for a few weeks. Parents did question how roller coasters connected to US History, and many thought we would get further behind in finishing the required curriculum, but we did fine!

The main lesson that I think most of the students got out of it was that it was hard...and they worked hard at it. Grit and perseverance were definitely the biggest takeaways from this activity, and I absolutely feel blessed that I was able to see the prideful moments when the marble made its way through their coaster for the very first time. In fact, my favorite reflection was a from a student that coined the term "smile glue" after she finalized her coaster. Check it out at http://bit.ly/smileglue.

In early December, we had an Explorer Roller Coaster Expo. I had reflections posted from students about the experience, as well as filled the cafeteria tables with the coasters. Some of the coasters were not completed, and that was OK. Some parents helped the students work on it during the Expo, and it was awesome to see the problem solving that went into it. Parents that attended the event got it, and many of them came up to me and shared the joy the event brought out, as well as how excited their kids were each and every day about social studies. In fact, some students even shared that they would lie in bed in the morning visualizing what they were going to work on for their coaster each day. How cool is that! Do you think most students lie in bed thinking about most classroom activities...probably not! I knew paper roller coasters were a keeper activity!

Since then I have taught 3rd grade, so I have had to modify the way I do coasters. This past year we created Book Club Coasters, and students created a coaster to connect with the book they read in series book clubs. It still took a few weeks working on it here and there during reading, but it was neat to see that third graders were able to figure things out and build their own coasters. Of course, I did have to help out with some of the elements again, but that was OK.

Other ideas that I think will work with coasters include:

- Create a coaster that explores a body system.
- Create a coaster that works as a timeline in history.
- Create a coaster that retells a story the student has written.
- Create a coaster that highlights a character in history or a book.
- Create a coaster that demonstrates a life cycle.

With the success of the Native American Makerspaces and the Explorer Roller Coasters, I knew I had to be more intentional with other units and making. For Colonial America, we had a Colonial Christmas Makerspace the last two days before winter break. Students sewed small pillows, dabbled in tinsmithing, made God's Eyes, and were able to do other things I found online. After finishing sewing a small pillow, one of my student's said, "I have never been so proud in my life!"

I replied, "Really? Your proudest moment ever?"

She replied, "Well...as far as school goes. I have never been this proud." Side note...this is a very successful, intelligent student who typically gets A's on her tests and projects. I then asked her to elaborate more on her pride, and she reflected, "This morning I didn't know how to sew. I learned how to sew and made this. I can sew now!" The pillow was a gift for her parents. I so hope they accepted the pillow and first try at sewing with the same excitement. It reminded me of the power of maker experiences. Regardless of what the project is...no matter how big or small, students get a strong sense of accomplishment and pride by learning new skills and making. Pride that I don't necessarily see when learning skills that we traditionally teach in the curriculum.

For the American Revolution, our class tried out green screen technology, as we created parodies covering the events leading to American Revolution. Students broke up into groups that included a lyrics group, a background group, singers, actors, prop makers, costume makers, and film crew. They used many things from our makerspace to build props and costumes. You can find an example of one of our parodies at http://bit.ly/greenscreenparody.

When learning about the Sons of Liberty and the liberty poles that were used to announce meetings, we found a great activity online that allowed kids to work in groups to build the tallest liberty pole using materials like straws, paper clips, and other common materials. The students really enjoyed this STEM-based challenge, while learning about the purpose of the liberty pole.

Overall, there are many, many ways that you can incorporate making into the curriculum. I would suggest thinking about one of the most boring lessons you typically teach (come on...we all know we have them) and try to create a maker experience that can help your students become more connected to their learning.

MAKE-ing a difference

Overall, allowing your students to discover their passions through making is one of the best things you can do. It allows students to experience learning through a whole new lens and really does engage them in ways a worksheet or notetaking never will. The motivation kids have to go deeper with concepts and possibly extend their learning on their own, comes from the power of making! So, I encourage all of you to try and **MAKE** a difference with your students and **MAKE** the curriculum come to life in an engaging way! Good luck and please reach out to me if you have any questions!

Here is a photo that was done professionally.

About the Author

Over her 20 years of being an elementary educator, technology has always been an area of focus Jennifer Bond's classroom. She enjoys leveraging her creativity with the various digital tools that technology and the web provides. She has embraced **BYOD** Days, Genius Hour, and the Maker Movement into her educational routine. She presents at state and national technology conferences on Edmodo, BYOD, Minecraft, Google for EDU, Computational Thinking, STEAM, Maker Ed and much more. Her most recent project has been being part of the www.Innovationclassroom.com team helping to provide PD with real classroom examples. She also blogs at www.TheEdTechCheerleader.com and can be found on Twitter @TeamBond.

CONVERGING STEAM TECHNOLOGIES: AN APPROACH TO INTEGRATING MAKERSPACE AND SMARTLAB IN THE CLASSROOM

Ella Marie

Ever-changing demands on STEM (Science, Technology, Engineering, and Math) education require all students are well prepared to participate in our global economy. Participation in a global economy is the pinnacle by which 21st-century skills propel students think about solutions as they are presented with everyday problems and challenges. Twenty-first-century skills of collaboration, communication, and critical thinking are vital for the next generation of diverse leaders (NSTA, 2011; DeJarnette, 2012). In our knowledge-based economy, the convergence of STEAM technologies such as Makerspace and Science Innovation Labs (or SmartLabs) have the potential to offer students real-world opportunities to connect science concepts to fields of science in diversely rigorous and creative ways.

Creative learning with makerspace

Learning manifests at many levels. Traditional learning has its place in the classroom, but in today's tech society, many educators are embracing techniques that infuse creative approaches to learning within a STEM context. In my case as a STEAM educator, Makerspace, which is a powerful set of techniques and approaches that allow students to embrace creative learning in both positive and exciting ways, was introduced by several Library Media Specialists within my school district to my middle school students.

Makerspace is a community-based workspace where individuals use tools to make, digitally design and learn techniques that also incorporate computer technology (Makerspace, 2018). Media specialists have a wealth of wonderful resources and are willing to share their expertise and knowledge with other educators (in or out of the classroom), which is how my students were able to experience an exciting STEAM project. The project leads to an I AM POEM collaboration with experienced Media Specialists, who worked with my 8th-grade science students. There, small groups personified a well-known scientist while embedding LEDs (Light Emitting Diodes) to illuminate important aspects of the scientists' accomplishments.

In this writing, the goal is to encourage other educators to think about converging Makerspace with a SmartLab concept (or other activities that put forth engineering design). Even if your school is not a STEM school, I hope by sharing my experiences as a middle school science educator who blends STEAM and creative learning with a variety of scientific concepts I will present options that extend into you expanding creative STEAM in the classroom.

The goal of the I AM poem was to allow students to creatively embrace the many accomplishments of science professionals ranging from IT (Information Technology) to the field of biological science through the integration of ELA (English Language Arts), writing and research. A well-structured framework of research questions was completed before the start of the activity (see Appendix A - Preparing for I AM POEM). The overall goal of the questions was to ensure that:

- State standards based on **NGSS** (Next Generation State Standards) and Common Core were integrated throughout the the process to encourage students to invest time and energy into this project;
- Students were captivated by the activity by engaging in the selection of a scientist to research and personify; and,
- Students were constantly thinking about ways to connect scientists with other science concepts such as physics (e.g., LED integration).

When the project was introduced into the classroom, I discovered that the students needed to build their understanding about Makerspaces and to see the long-term STEAM benefits, so I introduced my science students to the concept of a growth mindset (Mindworks, 2018) [see Appendix B - Information Presented to Students about Growth Mindset]. To our surprise, the project didn't seem to engage the students as expected. Working with our Media Specialist, we decided that we should try a "train-the-trainer" approach with a smaller group of students. It consisted of teaching students teaching students so a train-the-trainer website (via Google Classroom and setup by the Media Specialist) was developed to provide a support through the process. This group of students met each week with the Media Specialist to learn best practices and techniques, so they could later return to the classroom to offer their expertise and support to their peers.

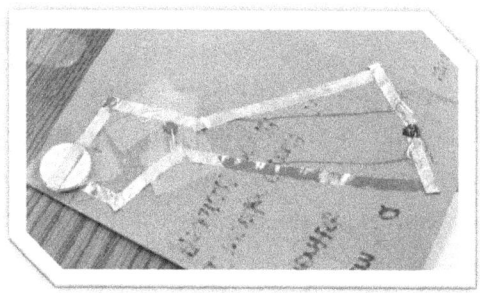

Students participated because I believed they would embrace an experience where they had the opportunity to make scientific connections across science and language arts. Overall, it would enrich their experience with STEM since the project extended over 5 days or more during the traditional science class time.

I really wanted the students to value the time, expertise and the knowledge of the Media Specialist so I decisively selected students who would 1) have a positive attitude going into the project; 2) appreciate the opportunity to teach others; ; 3) embrace being a team player and 4) and show a high level of intrinsic motivation.

The project had a positive impact on all of the trainers who spanned across a variety of classes such as Honors, Spanish and co-taught (co-taught classes are a combination of IEP (Individualized Education Plan) and students who have specific accommodations). Overall, the Makerspace activity provided a personal element for students because they were able to constantly think about the relationship between STEM in general and how they could aim toward similar accomplishments of the scientist they personified. It expanded students' thinking to the ideas that while they were making an inexpensive foldable book with multimedia components, they were also making lasting connections across academic disciplines of RELA (Reading Language Arts) and Math, which ultimately engaged them in a project that featured components of STEAM.

Simply put, by placing the technology in the hands of students, they experience the power to create, collaborate and connect in the classroom and as they think about a future STEM career.

Benefits of converging makerspace with SmartLab

Creative student activities presented from a Makerspace or SmartLab perspective captivates and encourages young people to embrace learning in new and interesting ways. A SmartLab platform encourages students to embrace a variety of activities that positively impact learning.

MAKERS IN SCHOOLS:
ENTERING THE FOURTH INDUSTRIAL REVOLUTION

Therefore, the technological convergence of Makerspace and SmartLab has the power to transform learning in unimaginable ways. Just as Makerspace provide opportunities to create a portfolio of their work, which includes reflections, photos, and videos, SmartLab purports the same philosophy.

SmartLab captivates students through engineering design and creativity where they are able to use a wide range of materials that encourage students to fully engage in computer graphics, digital communications, mechanics and structures, robotics and control technology, scientific data and analysis, software engineering and sustainability. With Makerspace, engineering practices (supported by NGSS) are put forth in every aspect and activities introduced by the Innovation Lab continues to lead students to engage in thinking about and building projects that put them in a role of becoming a future engineer.

For example, during one of the circuitry activities, students integrate Arduino to invent and work with programming circuits that merge with the engineering environment. With Arduino, students design and test circuits to control the blinking mechanism related to lights, audio, sensors and other advanced components. Converging Makerspace and SmartLab lessons and activities related to circuitry would present a power set of experiences for students to explore individually or as a team.

This is why STEAM benefits both educators and students. It is against this backdrop that I conclude with a hopeful message that if educators are searching for a simple yet creative way to encourage research relating to the districts STEM career pathways that directly relates to the science then consider working closely with a Media Specialist via video chat or Google Hangout. In essence, Makerspace opportunities are feasible for educators who want to inexpensively incorporate a STEAM activity that features cross-curricula components while SmartLab offers experiences that extend into building a project for longer periods of time. If educators consider a Makerspace project similar to the I AM POEM activity before integrating a program, then students will not only receive expose to scientists from different STEM fields but will be able to engage in a set of smaller activities that moves them one step closer to proficiently steeped in aspects of STEM.

Any educator who would like more information about the benefits of bringing Makerspace or SmartLab activities into the classroom, please feel free to email emarie1@cps.edu.

References

DeJarnette, N. (2012). America's children: Providing early exposure to STEM (Science, Technology, Engineering, and Math) initiatives. Project Innovation pp. 77-84(8).

Makerspace. (2018, July). Makerspace: make friends, make stuff, make a difference website. Retrieved on August 24th from https://www.make125.org/

Mindsetworks (2018, August). Decades of scientific research that started a growth mindset revolution. Retrieved on August 24th from https://www.mindsetworks.com/science/

National Science Teachers Association (2018, August). Quality Science Education and 21st-Century Skills NSTA Position Statement. Retrieved on August 3rd from http://static.nsta.org/pdfs/PositionStatement_21stCentury.pdf

About the Author

Ella teaches middle school science in a STEM school and for more than 6 years has encouraged students to think about science in creative and exciting ways. She currently teaches and collaborates with other educators who work with Makerspace and the Science Innovation Lab. She is in the process of completing National Board Certification - AYA: Science National Board Certification.

APPENDIX A:
PREPARING FOR I AM POEM

Students:

1. Once you have chosen the scientist you would like to research, you can start your research.

2. Work with your librarian, both school and local. The librarian should be able to help you with finding information you need and with citations.

3. As you begin your research and gather pertinent information, add relevant information you think will help you describe your choice of scientist. Use Step 1 Documentation #3 below to gather your information.

4. Cite your sources and list your citations under Step 1 Documentation #2.

ELLA MARIE

Step 1 Documentation	Step 2 Documentation	Step 3 Documentation	Step 4 Documentation	Step 5 Documentation
1. Who did you choose? 2. What resources did you use (at least 3)? 3. List your citations. 4. Your research (This can be a link to another Google doc, which can include images you want to draw, you might even use Google Draw (go to Insert>Drawing and try it out)	1. Insert images of accordion book. 2. What was difficult? 3. What was easy? 4. What would you do to make it better if you made another?	List the "I am"s as you create them, using your research to guide your understanding of your scientist.	1. Insert images of accordion book. 2. What was difficult? 3. What was easy? 4. What would you do to make it better if you made another?	1. Insert images of your simple circuit. 2. Insert images of your parallel circuit. 3. Where will you add your circuit and why? 4. What was easy creating a successful circuit? 5. What was difficult? 6. What would you do to make it better if you made another?

MAKERS IN SCHOOLS: ENTERING THE FOURTH INDUSTRIAL REVOLUTION

Begin work here:

Research a scientist using the following criteria for the project:

- Which century are the scientists from?
- What were their greatest challenges?
- Significant influences from childhood to adulthood?
- What were scientific needs from that time period?
- What were their greatest strengths? What helped them become successful?
- Some possible scientists to research:
    - Leland Melvin
    - Nikola Tesla
    - Jane Goodall
    - Mae Jemison
    - Rosalind Franklin
    - Hedy Lamarr
    - Virginia Apgar
    - Stephen Hawking

1. Read, write, think about the information presented. How will you use the information?
   The following materials will be used: scissors, tape, glue sticks, markers, rulers/cutting Mats, rolled up paper inserts, construction paper, and templates to design circuit.
2. Use your accordion book to design an I-AM poem that describes the scientist you chose to research.
   Simple line drawings for ideas: The Noun Project

Use your drawings to decide where the LED should go.

Practice making a parallel circuit. You will have to engineer your circuit in such a way that you can turn on LED on and off. Try it first then think about the last sentence. You might also consider using a battery holder.

Questions you should answer as you research your scientist:

1. First, middle and last name
2. Image of scientist
3. Country of birth
4. In which century or centuries did the life of the scientist span? (examples: 1654-1725; 1956-?)
5. What scientific needs were evident during the scientist's lifetime?
6. What was the scientist's field of study?
7. Where did the scientist do his/her work? Where did she/he study?
8. What were the scientist's greatest challenges? (For example, were there physical challenges, language barriers, economic barriers, social challenges, religious barriers, etc.?
9. What or who were significant influences on this scientist? Think about their childhood, changes in their lives, etc.
10. Give a description, in your own words, of why you think the scientist is famous.
11. Give an explanation, in paragraph form, of how the scientist's accomplishments affected our lives.
12. What do you think were the scientist's greatest strengths that supported a successful career?

MAKERS IN SCHOOLS:
ENTERING THE FOURTH INDUSTRIAL REVOLUTION

13. Other important facts?

Materials and Tools

- Laptop
- Internet access

Digital resources:

- Britannica School
- Britannica ImageQuest
- CultureGrams
- EBSCOhost
- LINK Online Resources
- NBC Learn
- ProQuest Dissertations
- Rosetta Stone
- SAFARI Montage
- SAGE journals
- SIRS Decades
- SIRS Discover
- SIRS Knowledge Source
- TeachingBooks.net
- World Book
- MackinVia
- Abdo Digital
- Rosen Interactive eBooks
- SIRS Discoverer Nonfiction eBooks
- Tumblebooks
- TumblebookCloud
- TRUEFLIX

APPENDIX B:
INFORMATION PRESENTED TO STUDENTS ABOUT GROWTH MINDSET

Watch the videos below, then answer the questions below with your best thoughts in Google Classroom. To organize the time we have, you will need 24 minutes for watching the video and about 20 minutes to answer the 2 questions.

- Growth Mindset Introduction: What it is, How it Works, and Why it Matters 8:25
- How We Learn - Synapses and Neural Pathways on Vimeo 3:14
- Gatorade Commercial 2017 The Secret to Victory 2:11
- 4 Steps to developing Growth Mindset 3:54
- How the Brain Learns 3:37
- Firing Neurons | Cell Dance 2010, Public Outreach Video Winner 3:55

Write about a time you have used Growth Mindset:
(Type your answer here)

At 4 minutes in the first video above, beliefs surrounding Fixed Mindset and Growth Mindset are described. Knowing that none of us are perfect, how might you strive to improve your life by changing even a small part of your beliefs about yourself? Use the 4 ingredients the narrator begins to describe at 4:29 to help you identify where you might improve:

(Type your answer here)

THE CLASSROOM OR LIBRARY AS A MAKERSPACE

Jackie Gerstein, Ed.D.

Makerspaces, Maker Education, STEM (Science, Technology, Engineering, Math) and STEAM (STEM with the arts added in) are gaining lots of traction in Kindergarten through college level education. Articles, resources on social media, and conference presentations on these topics are proliferating at a rate such that most educators are now familiar with maker education.

Once again this school year, schools will be ramping up robotics programs and opening more makerspaces, according to the latest report from the New Media Consortium and the Consortium for School Networking. As for "important developments" on the horizon, makerspaces (first listed as a trend in the 2015 report) will pick up speed over the next one to two years.

As schools continue to foster 21st-century skills in students in order to prepare them for the demands of a global workforce, K–12 will see the adoption of more makerspaces and research efforts to surface best benefits and practices.

Furthermore, the report noted that "makerspaces were initially lauded for their role in stimulating interest in STEM fields," but now they are often viewed as conduits to STEAM education with more emphasis on the humanities, visual arts, dance, drama and other areas of the arts (Ravipati, 2017).

Makerspaces, like vocational shops and science labs, are great additions to schools. They often contain the tools, machinery, and technologies associated with making - 3D printers, laser cutters, vinyl cutters, CNC routers, and vocational technology machineries such as electric drills and electric saws. These are a great addition for educational institutions that can afford them.

Problems occur when administrators, educators, learners, and communities come to believe that maker education is synonymous with these specialized tools and spaces. The first problem is that they may be out of budget for schools especially those serving lower-income populations. Second, the regular classroom teacher or librarian may be intimidated at the thought of using these advanced tools and technologies. Finally, to prevent maker education from becoming the educational flavor of the month, administrators, educators, and libraries should not be seduced by these shiny, new high-tech tools. The longevity and sustainability of maker education will depend on making it feasible, approachable, and accessible to the masses of educators, librarians, and learners.

Public focus on maker education often centers on flashy technology, but it is more than just that. Maker education is about building educational experiences that are based in the real world, that allow student choice, and that achieve multiple objectives. Maker education can be used in a variety of ways and projects can be adjusted in scale or scope to meet individual class or student needs. The key to successful maker education implementation is finding project ideas that seamlessly integrate "making" into the lessons. In the end, maker education is all about providing engaging experiences for students that bring out the best in them in the form of problem-solving and determination (Sparkfun, n.d.).

Lina Pugsley (2016) further describes the makerspace as:

> A Makerspace is a place where someone could come to learn how to use a new tool or material in a new way, see what others are working on and/or explore and discover how to use that new material or skill in pursuit of an intrinsically motivated project. It's basically a place where you can make cool stuff... while learning through hands on experimentation... practicing creative problem solving... and persevering through challenges to reach your end goal.

MAKERS IN SCHOOLS:
ENTERING THE FOURTH INDUSTRIAL REVOLUTION

With these broader definitions and approaches to maker education, and with the realization that maker education does not have to be about the shiny, new toys; more school administrators, librarians, and educators may be willing to embrace maker education within their own work settings. A classroom or library can be at least partially transformed into its own makerspace, a space for powerful student learning by doing the following actions workable and realistic for most librarians and educators:

- Removal of Obsolete, Non-Flexible Classroom Desks (including the traditional teacher's desk)
- Spaces for Playing, Tinkering, Making, Collaborating, Discussing, Researching, Reflecting
- An Agile and Nimble Learning Environment
- Affordable and Scavenged Materials
- Materials Openly and Easily Available
- Materials and Activities to Spark Diverse Learners and Their Diverse Interests
- A Place and Space That Supports Chaos and Messiness
- Accessible, Low-Entry, High Ceiling Materials and Activities
- A Learning Environment Driven by Learner Choice and Voice

- The Space Screams of Fun and Engagement
- The Space Screams of a Maker Mindset Not the Stuff

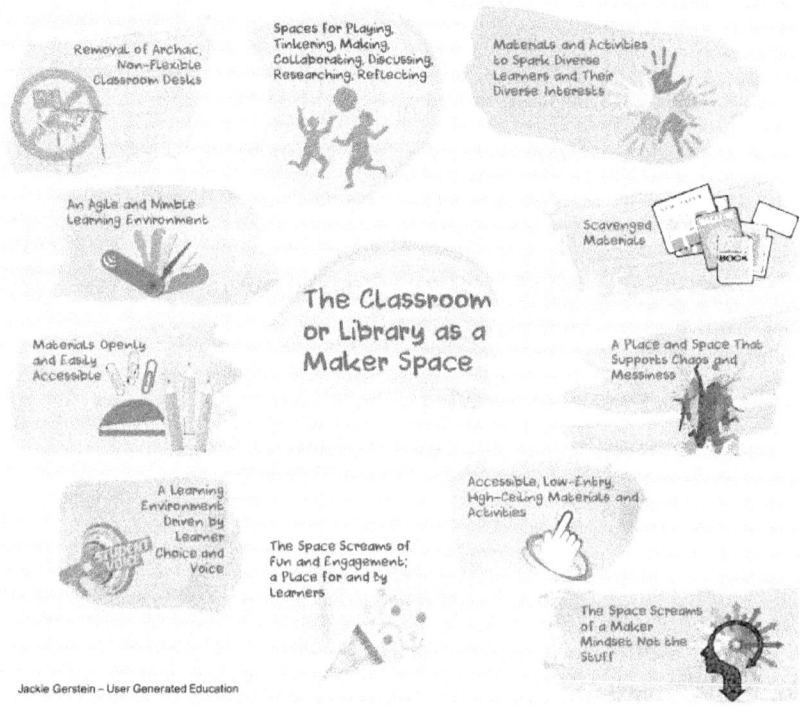

Removal of Archaic, Non-Flexible Classroom Desks

The image that often comes to mind about the classroom desk is one that features a plastic chair with chrome legs and a fiberboard tabletop that partially encloses a student's body. The first step for creating a classroom or library space that supports making is to get rid of these archaic pieces of furniture that probably were invented more for control than for productive learning.

The idea that students must be seated at desks working in rows to learn is quickly becoming archaic.

Technology and collaborative work environments are changing the design of learning spaces. Experts hope that the emerging paradigm will translate into improved learning spaces (Clifford, 2012).

An agile and nimble learning environment

The intentional use of flexible seating that forms agile and nimble learning spaces support the learning intentions typically associated with making education - creativity, innovation, iterative learning, collaboration, using resources in unique ways.

An agile learning environment is an educational playground that is intentionally designed to be adjustable, exchangeable and moveable. The learning space is designed to support idea generation, collaboration, and experimentation. Agile learning environments ultimately showcase how the design of a physical space, as well as the implementation of technology within that space, can shift how people communicate with one another.

The primary goal of an agile learning environment is flexibility. The furniture in the space, and the technology used within it are flexible so that it can be configured and re-configured to suit different approaches to learning and teaching. An agile learning environment has the ability to turn a static or 'dead' space into a dynamic space (Byrne, 2016).

With some creativity and flexibility, the practitioner can set up a unique, multipurpose space to serve the goals of making and the learners in that space as well as the multipurpose uses typically associated with libraries and classrooms. There are lots of resources that discuss flexible seating. Here is a ScoopIt aggregate of resources: http://www.scoop.it/t/flexible-seating-1.

Spaces for playing, tinkering, making, collaborating, discussing, researching, reflecting

Classroom educators and librarians may wonder how they might create these agile and nimble spaces for playing, tinkering, making, collaborating, discussing, researching, and reflecting. First and foremost, they need to develop an innovator's mindset, a mindset that thinks outside of the box of what a classroom should look, sound, and be like. Second, practitioners need to become intentional to help ensure that a full spectrum of making skills, attitudes, and knowledge is offered to learners. What will follow are educators and librarians who are creative, innovative, and resourceful in creating spaces that can offer a variety of learning activities.

Sure, there are some amazing products out there to create a futuristic, sleek active learning space like specialized seating, mobile desks and even hanging reading pods, but you don't have to invest in the expensive options. Add tennis balls to desk and chair legs so workspaces can be moved without a huge disruption or damage to floors. If you have a small budget to work with, purchase pillows and cubbies to create cozy spaces for independent reading. Or use whiteboard paint to make all sorts of surfaces "writable" (Team ISTE, 2015).

Affordable materials openly and easily accessible

In a learner-centered classroom environment, materials are displayed openly – being easily accessible by the learners on an as-needed-when-needed basis. Both of the elementary schools where I work have general consumables for educators (and I believe it's true for most schools): Xerox paper, butcher block paper, crayons, scissors, tape, markers, rubber bands, paper clips. These materials are stored openly in bins in cubbies for my learners to use when needed. Materials such as these can provide a foundation for making; brainstorming, prototyping, and reflecting and should be available for learners to use for their making activities without asking the teacher. Having them displayed can also spark learners' ideas. So, when a learner says something like, "I need some paper." (They ask because of their previous school experiences.) My comment back is, "Then go get it."

Using affordable and scavenged materials

There are so many avenues for acquiring materials for the classroom or library seeking to be at least a part-time makerspace. This can occur by using donor sites like Donors Choose or asking the students' families for materials but one of the best ways to acquire materials for making is scavenging.

Here is a list of affordable materials:

The Classroom or Library Makerspace: Getting Starting

Ask for donations; scavenge; apply for grants; look through supply & storage closets

❏ Cardboard	❏ Toothpicks	❏ Modeling Clay
❏ Shoe Boxes	❏ Popsicle Sticks	❏ Play-Doh
❏ Scissors	❏ Wood Scraps	❏ Pipe Cleaners
❏ Duct Tape	❏ Straws	❏ Old Battery Operated Toys; Computers; Appliances
❏ Paper (for sketching, origami, etc.)	❏ Rubber Bands	
	❏ Felt	
❏ Poster Board	❏ Fabric Scraps	❏ Aluminum Foil
❏ Markers	❏ Glue	❏ LEDs
❏ Paint	❏ Plastic Cups	❏ Copper Tape
❏ Brushes	❏ Nails, Nuts, Bolts, Screws	❏ Legos
❏ Yarn & String		❏ Discarded Books
❏ Greeting Cards	❏ Magazines	

Jackie Gerstein, Ed.D. – User-Generated Education

Once educators open themselves up to all of the possibilities of making, they will find free materials everywhere – cardboard at stores; recycled plastic bottles at school or the local recycling center; the storage closet at school where all of the old science kits are stored (I've found them at every school where I work) with all kinds of making supplies; old technologies and appliances for learners to take apart and build new inventions.

MAKERS IN SCHOOLS:
ENTERING THE FOURTH INDUSTRIAL REVOLUTION

Materials and activities to spark diverse learners and their diverse interests

As previously discussed, the maker education and makerspace movements are way too often symbolized by the machines: 3D printers, laser cutters, high tech components (Raspberry Pi and Arduino); and way too often it is white males who are attracted to these devices and technologies. "According to a 2015 study by members of the Maker Education Initiative, white males are the primary users of most makerspaces" (Dubrow, 2015).

In order to respect the diverse learners represented by gender, age, ethnic and racial background, then first, the definition of making needs to be expanded. As Adam Savage of MythBusters fame noted in his 2016 Bay Area Maker Faire talk:

> What is making? It is a term for an old thing, it is a new term for an old thing. Let me be really clear, making is not simply 3D printing, Art Lino, Raspberry Pi, LEDs, robots, laser and vinyl cutters. It's not simply carpentry and welding and sculpting and duct tape and drones. Making is also writing and dance and filmmaking and singing and photography and cosplay. Every single time you make something from you that didn't exist in the world, you are making. Making is important; it's empowering.

It is invigorating, but why? There are lots of results that are good that come from making. We improve the world around us. We show people how much we care about them. We solve problems, both personal and societal (Lomasney, 2016).

With this expanded definition of making, it follows that the activities and materials in the classroom or library should reflect the diverse learners and their specific interests. Making in the classroom or library can include, but not limited to: drawing, painting, paper crafts, sewing, sculptures out of Play-Doh or modeling clay or recycled materials, building with Legos or Kiva planks, creating with Web 2.0 tools, photography or videography, writing, and/or composing music.

A place and space that supports chaos and messiness

Traditional classrooms and libraries are often marked by students at their desks completing their learning tasks quietly and independently with as little movement of possible. This is the opposite of what happens in a making environment. The classroom or library, as a makerspace, becomes loud, seemingly chaotic and messy, but authentic and engaged learning is often messy during making.

Learning is often a messy business. "Messy" learning is part trial and error, part waiting and waiting for something to happen, part excitement in discovery, part trying things in a very controlled, very step by step fashion, part trying anything you can think of no matter how preposterous it might seem, part excruciating frustration and part the most fun you'll ever have. Time can seem to stand still – or seem to go by in a flash. It is not unusual at all for messy learning to be ...um ...messy! But the best part of messy learning is that besides staining your clothes, or the carpet, or the classroom sink in ways that are very difficult to get out ... it is also difficult to get out of your memory (Crosby, n.d.)!

When the library or classroom supports a makerspace, the librarian or educator needs to accept, to embrace messiness and all of that it entails. Things in the space are going to get messy.

Accessible, low-entry, high ceiling materials and activities

When discussing technologies to support learning and education, my mentor Seymour Papert often emphasized the importance of "low floors" and "high ceilings." For a technology to be effective, he said, it should provide easy ways for novices to get started (low floor) but also ways for them to work on increasingly sophisticated projects over time (high ceiling) (Resnick, 2016).

I do conference presentations where I have educators and librarians make paper circuits and Gami-bots. The success rate for these projects is 100% which translates into low entry into making (I took the liberty to change low floor to low entry). At one of my recent workshops, one teacher made the following design out of her paper circuit which says, "The moment you realize you can be a maker."

Similar materials can also be the foundation to create a high ceiling or more complex activities such as advanced art projects, most complex paper circuit projects, use of more advanced maker technologies.

A learning environment driven by learner choice and voice

The bottom line of setting up a learning environment based on the tenets typically associated with making is that learner voice and choice are enhanced. When choice and voice are intentionally built into learning, then school and education work.

> School works when students have opportunities to produce quality work about issues that matter. Education works when people have opportunities to find and develop unaccessed [sic] or unknown voices and skills. Audre Lord poignantly describes this "transformation of silence into language and action [as] an act of self-revelation." Opportunities for flexibility and choice assist learners in finding passion, voice, *and* revelation through their work (Block, 2014).

The space screams of fun and engagement; a place for and by learners

Piaget famously noted that play is the work of children and I have the belief that all humans maintain the sense of wonder of a child. Embedding fun into making; into learning in general increases engagement, joy, creativity, innovation, and collaboration.

> In our test-driven educational world of today being on task and on time in many schools leaves little time for play. Lunch periods have been shortened and days and years have been lengthened in an apparent quest to make our students into perfect little technicians, automatons who can react specifically in isolation to a set of pre- set stimuli in a consistent and certain way. Little room is left for the unexpected or the un-planned in our modern classrooms.

It is a strangely disastrous way to prepare our children for a future where it appears that the only constant will be continual change. By play, I do not mean little league, dance, or any other adult controlled activity. It must be kid controlled, kid directed, and kid policed for real learning about life to take place. Is it possible that our current infatuation with the concept that spending more time on something will make it better is so logical and easily observable and testable that just as logic and observation has in the past it might make people believe that the Earth is flat? (Teachosaur, 2012).

Fun can be felt, seen, experienced as soon as learners and visitors walk into the space. I love watching the faces of visitors when they enter my own classroom. They light up as they see my sofas, chairs, lamps; making supplies in cubbies in the back of the room; and most of all, my learners' work such as LED lit on student-generated posters hanging on the wall, paper roller coasters in-process of being made, and Lego creations on the Lego wall.

The space screams the maker mindset not the stuff

The battle cry of educators using educational technology is that the pedagogy needs to come before the technology. I am baffled, then, why I go to educational technology conferences and find so many sessions on the technology, e.g., 60 apps in 60 minutes. The same seems to be true for the maker movement these days. Practitioners talk about the maker mindset and then speak of the shiny new toys they use without talking about the context – of what skills and knowledge students learn from it. For example, with the 3D printer, they might talk about the Yoda they made, and I say, "So what?" It really is about having a maker mindset, not about the shiny, new maker tools. It's about the making process; about the engagement, creativity, innovation, struggles to complete a difficult task, the sense of accomplishment. A cardboard box, for example, can become a chariot, rocket, robot, marble run, Foosball game, dollhouse, Hot Wheels track, house, fort, castle, game.

> We must exercise the discipline to refrain from attaching too quickly to an idea just because it's new. Making is no exception, so to truly prepare ourselves to be successful in this new venture, let's be sure we set our students up to have the right mindset to be courageous innovators (Pierret, 2016).

With a maker mindset and some of the strategies outlined above, any classroom or library can become a makerspace.

References

Block, J. (2014). Student Choice Leads to Student Voice. Retrieved from https://www.edutopia.org/blog/student-choice-leads-to-voice-joshua-block

Byrne, P. (2016). The primary goal of an agile learning environment. Retrieved from https://www.school-news.com.au/teaching-resources/the-primary-goal-of-an-agile-learning-environment/

Clifford, L. (2012). Learning Environment: 20 Things Educators Need to Know about Learning Spaces. Retrieved from https://www.opencolleges.edu.au/informed/features/20-things-educators-need-to-know-about-learning-spaces/

Crosby, B. (n.d.) Learning is messy quotes. Retrieved from http://www.learningismessy.com/quotes/

Dubrow, A. (2015). Transcript: Adam Savage's 2016 Bay Area Maker Faire Talk. Retrieved from http://www.tested.com/art/makers/572766-transcript-adam-savages-2016-bay-area-maker-faire-talk/

Lomasney, K. (2016). Democratizing the Maker Movement https://www.huffingtonpost.com/aaron-dubrow/democratizing-the-maker-m_b_7960540.html?ncid=engmodushpmg00000004

Pierret, J. (2016). 6 Must Haves for Developing a Maker Mindset. Retrieved from https://www.edsurge.com/news/2016-06-06-6-must-haves-for-developing-a-maker-mindset

Pugsley, L. (2016). Makerspace 101. Retrieved from http://keepingcreativityalive.com/2016/10/maker-spaces-101/

Ravipati, S. (2017). Report: Makerspaces, Coding, Robotics Pick Up Momentum in Schools. *THE Journal*. Retrieved from https://thejournal.com/articles/2017/09/05/report-makerspaces-coding-robotics-pick-up-momentum-in-schools.aspx

Resnick, M. (2015). Designing for wide walls. Retrieved from https://design.blog/2016/08/25/mitchel-resnick-designing-for-wide-walls/

Sparkfun. (n.d.). Maker Education. Retrieved from https://sparkfuneducation.com/what-is-maker-education.html

Teachosaur. (2012). "Play is the work of children".... J. Piaget. Retrieved from https://teachosaur.wordpress.com/2012/02/20/play-is-the-work-of-children-j-piaget/

Team ISTE. (2015). Turn your classroom into an active learning environment. Retrieved from https://www.iste.org/explore/articleDetail?articleid=527

About the Author

Dr. Jackie Gerstein's byline is, "I don't do teaching for a living. I live teaching as my doing . . . and technology has amplified my passion for doing so." Dr. Gerstein is the author of The Educator as a Maker Educator. She teaches gifted elementary students, elementary- level maker summers camps, and graduate-level education technology courses in educational technology for Boise State, Walden, and Western Governors' Universities. Her background includes a strong focus on experiential and adventure learning, which she brings into her teaching. Maker Education fits naturally into this 21st-century version of experiential education. She believes that a major responsibility of a 21st-century educator is to share ideas and resources. As such she Tweets at https://twitter.com/jackiegerstein and blogs at https://usergeneratededucation.wordpress.com.

Section III: Practical Ideas for Makerspaces in Education

This last section brings us to the HOW. How can we bring the maker movement into our schools when funding is very limited? What are some "blueprints" for integration into your specific setting? The authors have shared ideas here, and invite you to share YOUR ideas (links at the end of this book) with others. Let us join forces to bring this important work into our learning spaces.

- **Bring the Maker Movement to Your School** by Barbara Liedahl
- **Making Something Out of Nothing** by Brian Costello
- **From Storyboard to Silver Screen** by Debbie Bohanan
- **Green Screens as Makerspaces** by Martine Brown
- **Go Green: Better Yet, Go Green Screen!** by Michael DuBose
- **Color Me Happy** by Katie J. McNamara

BRING THE MAKER MOVEMENT TO YOUR SCHOOL - ONE BOX AT A TIME!

Barbara Liedahl

Background

    21st Century Skills are deeply infused in the Common Core, Next Generation Science Standards, the National Core Arts Standards, the ISTE Standards for Students, and others. We see a nationwide push for more cross-curricular Science, Technology, Engineering, Arts and Mathematics (STEAM) activities in our schools. Computational thinking, coding, and programming activities are now included in school curriculum guides, not just in the upper grades, but also at the elementary level. Educators are involved in evaluating, re-aligning and developing new materials to more closely match the new standards - for all content areas. Creativity, critical thinking, collaboration, and communication are skills we all need to be members of society today. In education, we are experiencing a period of great growth and adjustment to more effectively meet the learning needs of our diverse student population.

    From these efforts, we are seeing a rebirth of the maker movement! Making and tinkering are coming back to our classrooms. Teachers are developing learning activities around topics and problems that are relevant to their students. Students are reverse-engineering old technology to see what's on the inside, and then re-purposing some of those parts to solve new problems. They are busy collaborating and reaching out to experts for guidance. They are revising, testing, and reworking their inventions to creatively solve the problem before them. This maker mindset is becoming the new normal in many of our schools.

Research shows that hands-on, engaging, and rigorous learning activities including those developed through making are highly effective in developing 21st Century skills. The maker movement is growing in our schools because educators are embracing once again that "to understand is to invent." In making, the active learner is "at the center of the learning process, amplifying the best traditions of progressive education." Schools are investing millions of dollars in building state-of-the-art makerspaces, equipped with expensive tools, materials, proper ventilation, and project ideas.

The problem

All this making is a good thing, but is it available for ALL students? Unfortunately, not all schools have the resources needed to build, staff, and maintain a makerspace. If hands-on, minds-on learning is essential, and we want ALL students to have access to rich learning opportunities, is there a way to bring the makerspace and the maker mindset to our students without the expensive tools, equipment, materials, and staff to maintain the program? How can we bring making to our classrooms without breaking the bank? How can we make these learning strategies available to all students?

The solution is in the box

We propose a solution to that problem: A Makerspace-in-a-Box. Our home-grown version of a Makerspace-in-a-Box is a collection of several easy-to-access boxes, each containing challenging prompts, tutorials, resources, and various inexpensive materials relevant to the challenge. Available in a classroom as a center, set up in a corner of a school library, or even available to "check out" like a library book, these clever boxes bring the makerspace and the maker mindset to the classroom, affordably.

This solution comes with one caveat: These boxes fulfill a need to get students making right away. That is a good thing, but it is not the end. We suggest using them as a beginning step in the path toward more complex maker activities. Both you and your students have to start somewhere, and we think this is a good place to start.

How does it work?

Details for each box can be found on our website: http://bit.ly/artfulmaking. Prompts and resources for various maker activities are developed for the following categories:

- Paper Engineering - Paper Circuits and Accordion Books
- eTextiles
- Felting
- Coding
- Physical Computing with Makey Makey, LittleBits and LilyPad
- Soldering

This list is not in any particular order, though beginning with Paper Engineering and/or eTextiles has proven to be a good starting point into the world of making in schools.

Paper Engineering

Starting with paper, a coin cell battery, copper tape and a light-emitting diode (LED), students can "illuminate their thinking." A simple challenge to illuminate a part of a written poem, drawing, or even a journal entry gets the students thinking and creating, while also writing, composing, and simply learning to activate online resources including tutorials or other supports. Please visit this web page to see the online resources we gathered for paper circuits: http://bit.ly/artfulpapercircuits.

Delving more deeply into paper engineering, we've developed a project built around an Accordion Book. Visit this page for more details: http://bit.ly/accordionGMAIL. In our example, we used ReadWriteThink's template for the "I Am" Poem to complete a character study of Juliet from Shakespeare's tragedy, *Romeo and Juliet*. The LEDs illuminate various lines in the poem.

This learning activity touches on learning standards in language arts, media arts, and **STEAM**. Some teachers have adapted the activity to apply to learning goals in other content areas. For example, one of our teachers had her students conduct research on a chosen scientist and compose an "I Am" poem from the perspective of that scientist. It was a real treat to watch how excited the students were to work on their projects.

With paper circuits, the potential for learning that "sticks" is high. The students are engaged, and they persevere when something doesn't work right, asking their peer-scholars for ideas and working together to solve problems.

eTextiles

Back when we were just getting started with this whole maker idea, I had an idea to make an ID Badge or brooch using felt material, a sewable battery holder, conductive thread and an LED. As my colleague Susan Brown describes in her chapter, the idea was borne during a brainstorming/crafting session with some friends. We decided that this would be a good "kit" project for beginners - a sort of "birdhouse" project where everybody makes the same thing, allowing for some creative choices, something that, if directions are followed, students experience nearly instant success, regardless of prior knowledge.

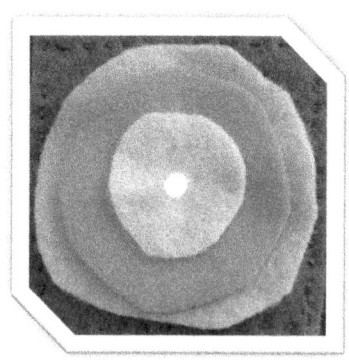

This eTextiles Maker Box's web page is http://bit.ly/etextiles. The eTextiles prompt is to create something that includes an LED that illuminates after sewing a circuit with conductive thread or connecting directly to the battery. Over the years, this project has been brought to ISTE poster and BYOD sessions, the National Art Educators Association's annual convention, classrooms and makerspaces around the country! It has also led to incredible new works of art by people interested in developing the art and design of integrating technology into works of media art, myself included.

Felting

Several years ago, I volunteered to participate in a Mini Maker Faire in the area, and I set up a booth for kids to create a simple wet-felted project in under 10 minutes (http://bit.ly/ArtFeltWoolHome). This project was popular at the Maker Faire, and we decided this could be something that could be done in school. The web page for this activity is http://bit.ly/artfelting. The challenge is to make a piece of wool felt using wool roving, soapy water, and a sandwich bag.

MAKERS IN SCHOOLS:
ENTERING THE FOURTH INDUSTRIAL REVOLUTION

The completed project, about the size of a coaster, could be integrated into an e-textile project, an extension of the pin/brooch they made earlier.

Getting the supplies (see our supply list), especially the wool roving, might be a challenge, but some online retailers sell it. I've purchased wool (three bags full!) at the annual Maryland Sheep and Wool Festival, directly from the farmers or already cleaned and combed from the many vendors at the festival. Extensions for felt-making abound: the science of how wool actually becomes felt; the insulating and water-resistant properties; where felt is used in everyday items; and much more. Who knows, you might end up with students who love the material so much that they go on to become world-renowned fiber artists!

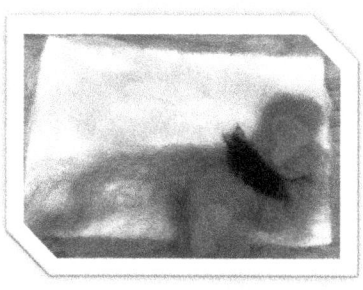

Coding

We have a coding box too. Our http://bit.ly/artfulcoding web page provides some links to online coding programs that students, young and old can access. Scratch, Scratch Jr., Code.org, and Microsoft MakeCode makes learning to code a lot of fun. These online activities can be completed using a browser - no software download needed, and they are platform-neutral. Even mobile devices can use the applications, in particular, Microsoft MakeCode. Participating in Code.org Hour of Code activities gives your students a "dip in the water" of coding. We recommend you try the activities listed on the coding web page above.

Physical Computing

Coding is fun and all, but it is much more fun if we can use it to make physical things move, blink, sense temperature, motion, humidity or light, or do whatever we want them to do with microcontrollers. Enter Physical Computing! Our box (http://bit.ly/artfulcomputing) contains links and materials for project ideas and challenges using Makey Makey, the LilyPad Protosnap Development Board, Little Bits, the Micro:bit and the ChibiChip from Chibitronics. This box is perhaps the most expensive of them all, but it contains the most potential for development of cool robots, gadgets, garments, and science projects.

MAKERS IN SCHOOLS:
ENTERING THE FOURTH INDUSTRIAL REVOLUTION

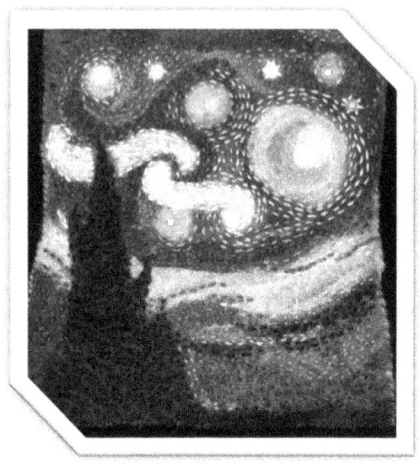

Depending on your available resources, any of these microcontrollers can be integrated into the eTextiles and Paper Engineering projects from above. Simple machines, automata, randomly twinkling lights, and anything else you can imagine can be developed by students with a little grit, ingenuity, and determination.

Soldering

Last, but not least, we have our Soldering box: http://bit.ly/artfulsoldering. We have a few projects listed on the web page that are easy for students to create while developing their soldering skills. Soldering paper circuits that are made with copper tape makes the connections more secure and reliable, especially if the project is manipulated in any way by the user. Creating a night light inside a jar (http://bit.ly/MiniFlipLight) that illuminates when the jar is turned upside down requires some soldering to secure the components, is not too difficult for students to manage.

However, soldering is perhaps the most dangerous activity so far in our Makerspace-in-a-Box lineup. That should not stop you from developing your soldering center. When students have developed the confidence in their abilities to learn and follow safety rules, they are capable of handling "grown-up" tools responsibly and without harm to themselves, others, and property. It just takes some careful scaffolding. We suggest you create a way for your students to earn a "soldering skills" badge by completing some training and passing an assessment that proves they know the skills needed to operate the equipment on their own.

Reflections and practical applications

We have shared our Makerspace-in-a-Box with educators for several years and have learned it is important to revise, adapt, and reflect on the success of this concept with students. Teachers have helped us tweak our idea and build upon new ideas, and we continue to do so. We think this is one way to bring a maker mindset and maker activities into your classroom, enabling all students to engage with the processes and the materials, and not costing a fortune.

Here is some advice we have gathered that will help you bring these ideas into your classroom:

14. Start small. Start with one box that seems the most relevant and interesting to your school or class. Consider piloting the idea with a small group of students.
15. Use whole-group instruction to introduce the students to the boxes, perhaps making one of the simple paper circuit projects with the whole class. The students will learn how to use the box, the

instructions and materials contained within, and how to visit online resources for tutorials and supports.

16. Store the boxes in a visible place in your classroom, and dedicate a location (a center) for the students to rotate into individually, or in small groups.

17. Develop a system for students to store their works-in-progress between sessions. You could display those in-progress projects on a shelf with a brief description of the project written by the student. Alternatively, the student could store their unfinished project in a resealable plastic bag labeled with their name.

18. Implement a system for using the "consumables" wisely. Have the students write a "proposal" for their project, listing the materials they will use, including how much/how many they need of each item, and getting your approval before they begin. Depending on the age group, you may need to measure out materials (the copper tape, for

example) according to the amount the student requested.

19. Encourage (or require) students to document their progress and self-reflect while working on their projects. Paper journals are great because they can sketch out their ideas before creating their projects, and then they can record the steps they took, write about what went well or went wrong, and list what they plan to do next. A simple "exit ticket" works well here.

20. Online portfolios are extremely valuable, especially if you want a record of their progress over time. Consider providing cameras and/or audio recorders for students to take pictures and describe their projects and then upload to their online folder. Pictures of their sketches and notes are also good to include. Over time, the students themselves can curate samples of their work and develop their own portfolios!

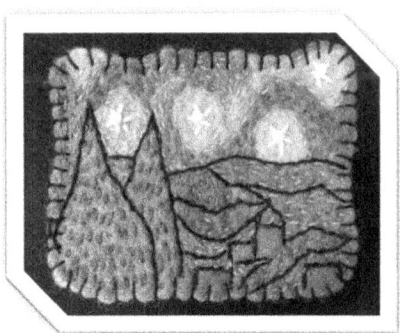

We hope that you give these ideas a try. Once you and your students are happily making fun yet challenging projects, you can expand your program to include additional types of projects and materials, and give the students even more voice and choice into what they want to make. Yes, you CAN bring the maker movement to your school - one box at a time!

References

About the book – Invent to Learn. (n.d.). Retrieved April 5, 2018, from https://inventtolearn.com/about-the-book/

Hack Your Notebook. (n.d.). Retrieved August 18, 2018, from http://www.nexmap.org/hyn-introduction/

Invent to Learn – Making, Tinkering, and Engineering in the Classroom. (n.d.).Retrieved April 5, 2018, from https://inventtolearn.com/

To Understand is to Invent - Constructing Knowledge with Piaget. (n.d.). Retrieved April 5, 2018, from http://etec512piagetconstructingknowledge.weebly.com/to-understand-is-to-invent.html

About the Author

Barbara Liedahl is a Media Arts Instructional Specialist in Maryland. Ms. Liedahl supervises Media Arts instructors, coordinates professional development, and supports all creative arts supervisors and teachers. Ms. Liedahl produces the Student Film Festival in her district. She serves on district and state committees and helped develop the Maryland State Department of Education's Media Arts State Standards. Ms. Liedahl has facilitated workshops and concurrent sessions at National and Regional Conferences on Media Arts, Arts Integration, STEAM, and Technology Integration. Embracing the Universal Design for Learning (UDL) framework, Ms. Liedahl promotes cross-curricular collaboration with technology and arts integration, including Science, Technology, Engineering, Arts and Mathematics.

MAKING SOMETHING OUT OF NOTHING

Brian Costello

It was the last day of school. I hadn't had many chances to talk to our new middle school science teacher since she had taken over in the winter, but we happened to talk for a few minutes that day. I heard her talking about makerspaces, so I struck up a conversation. I had been hoping to find someone to help me create a makerspace at our small school to expose our kids to the incredible benefits that they supposedly offered. I was on the verge of doing so when our previous science teacher left. Now, I had found another person who actually knew what I was talking about. In a few short minutes, we discussed the foundation of a plan. Where could we put it? We found an empty room across from the cafeteria, or we could use the library. There was an entire corner of the library that wasn't being used! All we needed was the OK. We knew there wasn't going to be anything in the budget for the makerspace, so we had to propose it as something that would cost the school nothing.

As we approached our Chief School Administrator (basically the Superintendent and Principal of our tiny school) we were expecting to get shot down hard. To our surprise, however, it didn't take much convincing. He was open to the idea but reiterated that we wouldn't have any funding. WE HAD A MAKERSPACE! Now what?

Where do we start? How do we decide what will be in the space? How will it be structured, run, managed? There was so much to figure out, and we were both leaving for the last day of school in just minutes. We discussed what needed to be done and quickly scribbled some plans and details on a piece of paper. Our journey had begun.

From nothing to something, with 0$ for the budget. We had so many challenges. If you are hoping to build a makerspace, or a fablab, or an entrepreneur sewer (ok that last one isn't a thing) I am happy to share the challenges and what I learned from the process.

Where do we begin?

This isn't your district mandating that makerspaces become a thing in every school, this is you deciding on creating an incredible learning opportunity for kids. So, how do we get the ball rolling?

Creating a makerspace takes a significant amount of upfront planning. Doing so without any funding requires thought into what you need to get started, how you will create excitement and the management of space and supplies. So, start with two essential questions:

Who are your users?

What do you want them to get out of the experience?

In our case, we were working with a K-8 population which we wanted to expose to more opportunities to create, problem-solve, and explore new technologies. It led to some unique challenges. Our students, especially our 5th-8th students hadn't spent a lot of time creating over their educational careers. For much of that time, they had been receiving the directions and never having to develop a product on their own. Younger students rarely have issues creating and making. It is still a genuine part of who they are as individuals. As kids spend more time in school (especially in school environments where using creativity and critical thinking to solve problems isn't the norm), they lose the imaginative touch that allows for strong maker culture. Our users were a diverse group in age and also exposure to any technology beyond a computer class.

To attract users, we knew we would need some flashy items to draw attention. Over the summer we raised funds through Donors Choose projects that saw us acquire two Sphero robots and a 3D printer. During the first few weeks, we reached out to our district's Home School Association as well. They provided us with funds to buy two Little Bits kits. We also reached out to the community for donations. We needed Legos, aging technology devices, and we took any arts and crafts donations we could get. All of this would begin as the starting point for our space. We had some flash, we had some digital and physical opportunities, and we had a space in which to work.

You may be wondering, "What do I buy?" Ideally, nothing. Leverage resources, ask for donations, basically do whatever you can to raise funds or materials. Regardless of how you get the funding, your purchases should focus on what will engage your students. Talking to your students to find out more about their interests is a good starting point. From there you can help create the stretch toward more high-end maker tools. What did my kids want? They wanted Legos, tools to take apart computers, and drones (i.e. Sphero). What they found over time was the amazing ability to combine the many objects we had in our makerspace to create something new.

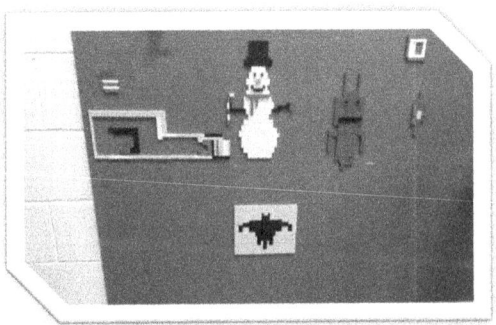

Despite being a small community, our early donations were still enough to get us started. We promoted the space by talking about it with kids individually and also at assemblies and other public gatherings of students. By our launch date, we had created a very basic space, but there are so many more things to successful makerspaces than just having stuff.

MAKERS IN SCHOOLS:
ENTERING THE FOURTH INDUSTRIAL REVOLUTION

Makerspace management

Sure, our new space seems basic, but comparing your new and developing space to some of those fully funded, long time successful spaces is unrealistic. If you are building this from zero, looking at the ideal makerspace is like envisioning the finish line of a marathon. Yes, it is where you want to be, but there is a long, challenging road between you and the end goal. Be realistic in your expectations about how your space will look, feel, and what your kids will be able to do based upon how well you know your users.

Managing your makerspace is extremely important. Who will have access to what and when? Do you have adequate, organized storage? Are your staff willing to bring kids into the space? Do you need volunteers?

All of these questions are important management questions in starting your school's makerspace. If you have someone in the space throughout the day, it changes how you can run your makerspace. In our case, we would only be available on certain days during lunch periods to run the space. We needed volunteers to have <u>the space</u> open every day. It was incredibly helpful, but at the same time, we had the significant challenge of not being available to assist classroom teachers who were interested in the space.

Storage is one of the most fundamental questions you will address in planning your space. Yes, storage. Makerspaces are messy (if this is a surprise to you, you may need to do some more research.) But, that mess should not impact the ability of kids to find tools, materials, and unfinished projects. Who has ownership of the projects? Are they community-based? If not, how do students store them during the process?

Finally, what is the culture in your building? Do teachers, students, or parents have any making background or experience? Our small district had some amazing external resources. We were able to bring in a parent to explain a computer hard drive to students and show them the parts that make them function. From that demonstration, we inspired a number of students to explore what they could build and create with the gears inside the hard drive and CD/DVD ROM as well as the discs, cooling fans, and high-powered magnets within the computers. Our teachers were still growing into the ideas for making, but many of our students had fantastic ideas and skills they were able to share with others. All of these things drive the decisions and also the creative spark within a new space.

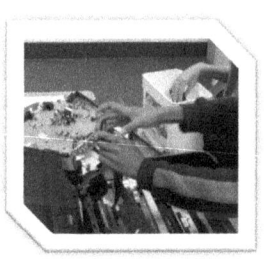

Learning to play

A huge part of successful makerspaces is developing a maker mentality in your school. One of our biggest struggles with staff and students was breaking through the mindset that play, failure, and building are not also learning. While many of you who read this book may think that is apparent, the concepts are not widespread throughout education in most places. Despite being a school where lots of positive changes had been made, and plenty of good teaching was taking place, the prevailing attitude toward building, making, and creating was that it wasn't a meaningful learning activity.

Play is our initial entry into learning. So much of what we learn in our early years is done through play, but upon entering formalized school, we shut down the concept of playing to learn. To truly create a strong maker culture, learning to embrace play, exploration, and struggles must be incorporated.

So how can we create this culture? How do we undo the years of formalization that has conditioned students to avoid failures and playing with their learning? It starts by encouraging students to wonder. Young minds are full of questions, curiosity, and wonder. Start engaging that wonder by taking time to hear what students enjoy. When students have questions, encourage them to find answers. Learn to "look it up," to test it out, or to tinker with it to find your solution.

Starting by encouraging people to find it for themselves is only the beginning. From there, kids also need to be empowered to build, create, and explore to learn. While we create the conditions for these in the makerspace, we must also expand upon them by helping our students connect their play/exploration to the concepts they have or need to continue expanding upon their creations and tinkering. Each exploration or creation will offer opportunities to extend into multiple areas of education.

If we hope to take our makerspaces to the level of self-sustainability, a strong maker culture needs to be in place. It won't be built overnight, but through continual, gradual pushing toward the goal of embracing play, tinkering, and wonder to learn.

Planning a sustainable space

So, you managed to create a successful makerspace. You started with only an idea of what the space might become, and it has morphed into a living, breathing space. You may have even convinced the powers that be to fund your space in the future. But, no matter how successful your makerspace has become, you will almost certainly face the reality that the "maker fad" will sooner or later come to an end. At some point, likely soon, the financial support for "Makerspaces" will dry up. But, the value of creating, exploring, playing, and building to learn will not stop being valuable. So, finding a way to preserve the incredible learning that happens in a maker environment should be paramount to any successful space.

Creating a sustainable space takes many forms. Several important features need to be in place to continuously fund and maintain your space. I remember awakening to this reality in discussion with Chris Aviles of Fairhaven Public Schools (@techedupteacher) where we discussed many of the tenants of his article (see References). Between the lack of money and the ever-changing landscape of education and education "fads" the Makerspace by name is going to disappear. So, step one to decreasing the chances you will lose the maker culture you hope to build, start by branding it differently. You don't have a makerspace, you simply have a learning space, so call it something else. My computer lab/makerspace/recording studio is referred to as the Fernwood Future Lab. Adam Juarez of Cutler-Orosi Joint Unified School District built the "Cardinal Innovation Center," Chris Aviles has the "Fairhaven Innovation Lab." Innovating and creating new things will never lose its value, but a makerspace will. Find something that will last beyond the maker craze that will lead you to sustainability.

Another step you can take toward sustainable spaces is to provide services for the school and community. As students become adept at tinkering, computer and graphing design, and more, their services will provide incredible connections for the community. It will also provide the opportunity for some self-funding. As students learn to take apart and put together technology components, they can begin to repair broken devices, reimage old computers, and clean hard drives. They can also provide services for local businesses creating digital media, setting up simple computer automation, and menu designs. Students can also contribute creative services if they become proficient at designing and printing objects. All of these small steps help create a space that has financial independence from the school's potentially volatile economic changes.

My final suggestion for creating a sustainable space is possibly the most important: gain the support of the families in the school community. Your local PTA/HSA, Parent's Club, Education Foundation or any other groups will help with funding, but more importantly, if the maker culture you are hoping to create becomes embedded in the fabric of the community, then you will find your space much more difficult to remove from the community. Talk to parents, invite them into your space, find community members that can interact within the space with kids. All of these lead to parental support and engagement. When it comes time to make important decisions for the district, having the support of influential parents is invaluable.

So, you are about to embark on an incredible journey of creation, discovery, and excitement. Creating a maker culture and having an innovative space will be challenging. You will have many obstacles to overcome, even more so if you are starting without the funding that typically comes with administrative support. Find people who will follow you in this endeavor and support you on this journey; you will need them. More than anything though, you will have more success and see more gains for your space and your students if you remember the most important thing: HAVE FUN!

References

Aviles, Chris. (November 11,2015). *The Makerspace is Doomed.* Retrieved from http://www.techlearning.com/blogentry/9979

About the Author

Brian Costello, the author of The Teacher's Journey and owner of BTC2Learn LLC, is a Google Certified Innovator & Trainer in his 10th year of teaching in Southern New Jersey. His career started as an instructional aide before going on to teach Kindergarten, 1st, and 2nd Grades for the past seven years. He now works as a middle school technology integration specialist. He is an avid writer, blogger, and Twitter user and has published two children's novels: Will McGill and the Magic Hat and Will McGill and the Costume Calamity. Brian was a spotlight speaker at Tech Rodeo and presents around the United States on topics including educational technology, leadership, communication, and professional development. He is also the creator of The Global Audience Project to help classes find, and be, authentic audiences for projects.

FROM STORYBOARD TO SILVER SCREEN

Debbie Bohanan

These days everyone seems to be an amateur videographer but how do you create an engaging video instead of a boring home movie that nobody wants to watch? If you have been around as long as I have, then you remember growing up and watching home movies. Whenever my grandparents came back from a trip, we were always subjected to long slide shows of desolate roads and vast countrysides. I might appreciate those more now, but as a kid, they got old real quick. Remember Mom taking videos on her 8mm film reel? The excitement of taking a trip back in time is quickly replaced when you watch a 6-year-old child swim the entire length of an Olympic sized pool. Do you know how long that takes? So how do we take advantage of the cameras in our pockets and create movies that will even keep our teenagers on the edge of their seat?

The first thing you need to do is start thinking in shots. This concept can be very challenging but can be mastered with a few simple tricks. When shooting a video, we need a subject, action, and cut. The same can be said when thinking in shots. The best way to get this concept across is to use a comic strip. Simply find your favorite comic in the Sunday paper, white out the dialog, and distribute it to your students. Tell the students they need to create the story and fill in the speech bubbles. Once the students have created their dialog, present their comics to the class. Discuss the story and each box in the comic and help the students realize that these are the shots in a very simple short film. By examining each frame in the comic, they will see the subject and what action was taken. As soon as the action is over, the comic moves to the next box. Congratulations on starting the process of changing their way of thinking so that each scene can be thought of in shots.

When you feel the students are ready to move on, introduce them to a basic storyboard. The easiest storyboard to create is by simply folding a piece of 8.5" x 11" copy paper in half three times to create eight sections. To do this, fold it in half, crease, then fold it in half again. Fold the paper in half one more time and use a ruler to go over the folds to make the creases more pronounced.

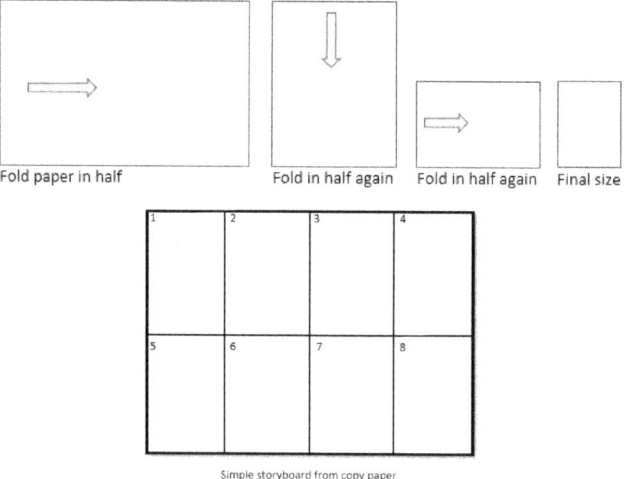

Simple storyboard from copy paper

Open the paper and use a ruler to trace over the lines and number the boxes. If you use the front and back side of your paper, you have 16 boxes available on your storyboard (8 on each side).

To begin completing your storyboard, use the outline of your project and break it down into shots. Ask your students to think about the last movie they saw. When they were sitting in the movie theater, what was the first thing that happened; the opening shot? Typically, it is an aerial shot that turns into an establishing shot. The aerial shot for New York City would probably take us over Central Park with the skyline in the background. If your classroom is like mine, you are probably lacking in the area of drones, making aerial shots difficult and challenging. If you have the technology, by all means, incorporate it for a stunning opening shot. The rest of us, on a small or non-existent budget, will typically start with an establishing shot. Establishing shots let your audience know your location and are typically filmed on ground level. To go back to the New York City location, the establishing shot could be on the street in front of the Empire State Building. Once the audience knows where the video is taking place, it's time to start your story.

Storyboards do not need to be fancy artwork that can be framed and hung on the wall. My storyboards are simple and contain some of the best stick figures in town. Remember... the point of the storyboard is to break your project into shots to assist the camera operator and director while filming.

You may want to add additional details to your storyboard. In this case, one that contains a few lines for direction or dialog may be helpful.

Storyboard with lines for dialog or directions

As your students become more comfortable with the storyboard, it will be helpful to the camera operator and director if you add shot types and camera movements to your storyboard. The most common shot types are an establishing shot, medium shot, close-up, two shot, and over the shoulder shot. The establishing shot, as I mentioned earlier, will help your audience determine the location of your video. Medium shots are the most common shots and include your subject from the knees up to the head. A close-up shot is used to show the emotions on your subject's face. When two characters have a relationship, the two shot is used to portray the subjects as friends, enemies, etc. The fifth shot is done over the shoulder of one subject. The idea behind that shot is that two people are involved in the conversation but the one speaking is the focus of the shot. Students can create a simple key using the first letter of each shot type and add it to their storyboard.

1 ES	2 MS	3 CU	4 TS
5 OTS	6 CU	7 MS	8 MS

Shot Types:
Establishing Shot: ES
Medium Shot: MS
Close Up: CU
Two Shot: TS
Over the Shoulder: OTS

Storyboard with Shot Type Codes

Remember that storyboards are tools to help visualize the story. Details help others understand your vision for each shot. The best way for students to determine if all the necessary parts of their shots are included in the storyboard is to give it to someone else who is not in their group. Ask yourself, "If I gave this storyboard to someone else, could they film my movie the way I want it to look?"

If your students are like my students, they will struggle to include all the necessary details. The reason is simple. They have the vision for their movie in their head and know exactly what it should look like. Unfortunately, they sometimes forget the most obvious details because they assume you know what is happening in each shot.

The solution to this problem lies in the making of a peanut butter sandwich. This was always one of my favorite activities as a writing teacher because it helps my students think about every detail. I am sure some of you have done this activity before, but for those of you who don't know what I am talking about, I will let you in on the secret of detail writing.

The first thing you do is ask your students to write down the directions for making a peanut butter and jelly sandwich. Tell them to include enough details that someone could use their directions and make a sandwich. For the demonstration, you will need a knife (plastic of course), a jar of peanut butter and a jar of jelly, a loaf of bread, and a plate.

Once the students have finished writing, ask a volunteer to read their directions for how to make a peanut butter and jelly sandwich. Typical responses usually start with put the peanut butter on the bread. So, you model this direction by putting the jar of peanut butter on top of the bag of bread.

The class will break out into laughter as they begin to see how details are very important if someone else is going to follow your instructions.

Continue with the directions as you drive home your point. Their details will definitely have your class rolling on the floor as you do exactly what they say without ever successfully making the sandwich. Encourage students to revise their directions and watch the details in their writing come to life.

Now that your students have a better understanding of details, have them review their storyboards and add any additional pieces of information to their story. Once the students are satisfied with their storyboards, select one for the class project. Make copies of the storyboard and distribute them to each group. The groups will be given the same resources and time constraints to film the project. Once all projects have been filmed, edited, and submitted, play them for the class. Share each project with the class but save the storyboard creator group's project for last. As each video plays, tell the students to compare it to the storyboard. Is anything missing? Does it appear to follow all the details on the board? When the final video plays, compare it to the other projects. What differences did you notice? Did the final project include anything that wasn't on the storyboard? Have the students discuss what elements should be included in the storyboard to create the project that matched the creator's vision.

To help students realize the value of a storyboard, check out the additional footage on Finding Nemo where they talk to the animators and show how the storyboards are created and organized before the movie is ready to be filmed. Some students complain about how long it takes to create storyboards, but when they see how much work is put into the storyboard for Finding Nemo, they feel better about the small scale of their project.

When you begin filming your movie, these three words are worth their weight in gold - subject, action, cut. Students need to take their shots from the storyboard and turn them into clips that capture the audience's attention while capturing the action. I had a student who wanted a shot showing two students walking into the school. As she set up the shot, she explained that she wanted to see them walking down the hallway but what she meant was ALL THE WAY down the hallway. I could have stopped her and told her that her scene was way too long, but I decided the most effective technique would be for her to see it during the editing process. I knew that somewhere in her clip was something she could use, so her efforts were not wasted.

MAKERS IN SCHOOLS:
ENTERING THE FOURTH INDUSTRIAL REVOLUTION

Returning to the classroom, she downloaded her clips and began editing. As she pulled her clip into her timeline, I asked her to play the clip and press the spacebar to stop it as soon as she was bored. After only 2.5 seconds, she had stopped the clip, looked at me and said, "Oh...Now I get it". She had to experience it for herself to learn and grow. Her next clips were much more concise, and she learned from her previous clip. To be successful and truly see the importance of a technique, sometimes we have to fail before we succeed.

Camera movements are going to come into play while filming your shots. Students need to determine if their shots are going to be on a tripod or handheld. Tripod shots offer a steady professional feel to your video. When shots are handheld, they have a slight jerky feel to them. Sometimes shots are low angles, and the camera may need to be lower than a tripod can go or even on the floor. Students will need to decide which method is best for the shot they are trying to achieve.

Panning and tilting are appropriate camera movements when tracking your subject. If they are walking down a hall, you can pan (move from right to left or left to right) as you follow them. Tilt (moving up to down or down to up) is a technique they may use for showing the size of a subject like a tall building. Tilt can also be used to guide the audience to a specific spot and then be followed by a medium shot on the action taking place at that spot.

If you are going to be moving the camera on location, you will want to make sure your camera is on a dolly (basically a tripod with wheels). This will produce a smooth sequence for your film.

The last type of camera movement that you may want to include is a zoom. Sometimes the only way to truly capture the action is to zoom in (get closer without physically moving the camera).

> **Camera Movements:**
> Tripod: T
> Handheld: H
> Pan: P
> Tilt: T
> Dolly: D
> Zoom: Z

    All of these camera movements are going to be important for the director and the camera operator and should be noted on the storyboard. Providing as much detail as possible will assist your students when filming to make sure the shot is captured exactly how they wanted it to look. This will also save time by avoiding having to go back into the field and shoot those shots again. In the industry, if you had to redo a shot, it would cost time and money, and it's important for your students to understand that.

    With the advancements in mobile devices, more and more people have access to a video camera and these techniques will help them go from amateur home movies to engaging videos that even a teenager will watch.

MAKERS IN SCHOOLS:
ENTERING THE FOURTH INDUSTRIAL REVOLUTION

About the Author

Debbie Bohanan is an innovative educator who loves teaching and learning. She shares that love of learning with her students and inspires them to be the best they can be. Teaching digital video to at-risk students has given her a platform to infuse creativity and technology while actively engaging her students utilizing project-based learning and gaming. Students apply the skills they learn in real-world applications giving value and meaning to their work. Digital storytelling and online learning platforms are evident in her room, and technology is clearly integrated into every aspect of her curriculum. She has presented at Discovery's Ignite Your Passion, FETC, and ISTE. Debbie holds a bachelor's degree in Elementary Education from Florida State University and a master's degree in Education Media Design and Technology from Full Sail University. She is a National Board Certified Teacher, Discovery DEN Star and Leadership Council member, Tech4Learning TIE, Microsoft MIE, and a Florida Digital Educator.

GREEN SCREENS AS MAKERSPACES

Martine Brown

When I first began the process of introducing green screen tech, I was slightly afraid. At the time I was teaching a ninth-grade college readiness course (AVID) and wanted my students to create a presentation that showcased different colleges. The goal was to have my students work collaboratively to create a mini college tour, where we would "tour" five to six campuses. Traditionally, my students would use the standard presentation program and share the findings after a few days of research. Having students create a slide presentation was easy for me as their teacher, and I felt confident that they could complete the task. That year though, I wanted to do something different, to challenge my students in a new way, and utilize the iPad cart in a way that would prepare them to engage in our district's 1:1 program that was rolling out the next school year. I took the risk in hopes that my students would grow, and I found that I grew as well.

MAKERS IN SCHOOLS:
ENTERING THE FOURTH INDUSTRIAL REVOLUTION

Classroom integration of green screens to "make"

The results of this lesson helped me gain confidence in integrating technology while also enriching my students learning of content and technical skills. When students first began to plan their presentations, I found that they formed their groups and used Google Slides to design their presentation. Since I was using this collaborative tool with students for the first time, I realized first hand that using the tool allowed students to work interdependently and made the assignment more attainable as a team. The real magic started when the students planned their storyboards and built their group videos. Immediately, the students began to talk out their plans and learn how to use the application. The students were moving around the room staging their backgrounds, building, constructing, and deconstructing. At different moments there were hushed tones as they explored ideas that they wanted to be unique to their group. I zig-zagged around the room and hallways facilitating and troubleshooting. I also realized that students felt empowered when they could teach me what they were learning. I made a point to say "Show me how you did that!" or "That is so cool! How did you figure that out?" The effect was a sense of ownership of their work and confidence that their team could do great work with new skills. Another unexpected outcome was that students began to coach each other as they developed their recordings. They helped one another with improving their posture, tone, and gave them immediate feedback to produce quality work. I think that this is what makes green screens as makerspaces such a powerful tool. When given time, opportunity, and flexibility in design, students are learning authentically in a way to promotes their ability to communicate, thinking critically and be creative.

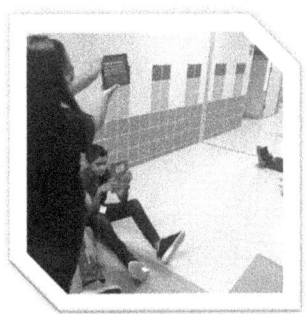

Green Screen App by DoInk

I learned about the Green Screen App by DoInk (2.99) from my district. To ease navigation in the app, I created a strategy called the hamburger technique. Since many students have experience with this concept as it relates to writing, I thought this would give the application some context that was relatable. The bottom "bun" is the background image, much like a newsroom, it is the weather map shown to the audience. The middle layer is the "meat" of the presentation, where the video is uploaded. Think of the weatherman who stands in front of the map. The background is the bottom layer, then apply the weatherman on top, as you would the hamburger meat. The top layer is the top "bun" for any other videos or images you would like to include. Once the layers are in place, move the Chroma icon to adjust the color setting, and your video is ready to preview or save. As students gained confidence in using the app, they were able to use this baseline to guide their work.

Instructional coaching and green screen tech

As I began to work as an instructional coach, I wanted to share with colleagues the impact of using this type of technology in their classroom. I discovered that the most significant concern was that the technology may be too complicated and time-consuming. To overcome these challenges, I found that creating mini maker stations during staff development was a great way to introduce the tool and have cross-curricular discussions regarding the relevance of green screen technology for the classroom. I also set up these mini spaces during local Edcamps to promote the concept of a creative media-based makerspace.

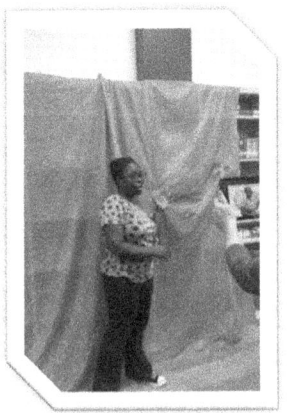

The third strategy that I used to build teacher capacity with the Do Ink app was to hold holiday themed sessions for teachers and students. Our campus library has a set of iPads and teachers signed up their classes to learn how to use the app as well as gain tips on guidelines related to copyright and digital citizenship. These sessions lasted 30-40 minutes, and by the end, students had the technical skills to perform content related tasks.

Everyday tips and resources

To boost creativity, have students use tools like Adobe Page, Piktochart, and Canva to create their own images, designs, and background.

Pics4learning- Has a listing of thousands of images categorized by content. (Citations can be copied and pasted straight from the website.)

Bitable.com - Create short videos and photos using their stock content.

Check with your school librarian for resources available for students. Britannica Image Quest is one resource that our district provides schools.

The Makerspace for Education website also has a ton of resources to help teachers get started with empowering student creativity using green screen technology.

About the Author

Martine (MAR-TEEN) Brown is the Ready 1:1 Instructional Coach for Garland Independent School District. With 14 years of experience in education, Martine has worked with students as an English Language Arts and AVID Elective Teacher. In her current role as an instructional coach, she provides school and district level professional development, job-embedded support for effective strategies of 21st-century learning, and models effective instructional and digital strategies with teachers. In her free time, she enjoys running and participating in 5k races. In 2016, she ran her first 1/2 marathon. She also likes to style hair, cook, dance, spend quality time with her husband Kevin, and children Devin, Maxwell, and Charlotte. Her mantra is Every Student Counts, and it is her mission to be a catalyst for change in education.

GO GREEN: BETTER YET, GO GREEN SCREEN!

Michael DuBose

Why go green?

The use of green screen technology in *all* classrooms is a simple way of transforming the learning environment into an incubator for both creative thinking and much-needed alternative methods of assessment. Not for students only, but as Education Technology Specialist Hanna Shekhter of Brauser Maimonides Academy in Fort Lauderdale, FL puts it, this fun technology gives teachers a way to "transport students to another location or time."

Our current video-driven generation of students would be right at home placing themselves on-screen at a famous Civil War battlefield, describing the event instead of droning out memorized facts about history.

(These images have been placed on the green screen background using *TouchCast Studio*. The student could then annotate the image, provide narration about the event, or use it for a live or recorded discussion.)

What about this... the STEM project that, due to a school's limited resources, may not have the hands-on items needed for demonstration purposes? Move over Bill Nye...green screens to the rescue!

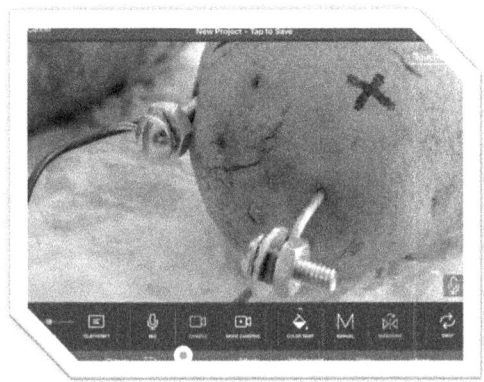

Whatever the classroom project may be, with the use of one of my favorite iPad apps, *TouchCast Studio*, students can *Go Green.* Using this app, students record their science project "live" from Thomas Edison's lab; screen capture their solution to an Algebra problem, with audio explanation; or demonstrate their understanding of "Curl Down and Up" or "Leg Swings" for their Modern Dance class, while "on stage" at The Metropolitan Opera Lincoln Center. Any projects such as these can easily be used as an alternative assessment, allowing students to have fun while completing them.

My experiment

My passion for teaching outside the box exploded once again as I watched the success of a recent experiment that I conducted with seventh and eighth-grade middle school classrooms. In my Creative Arts Technology classroom, I set up six green screen stations, some mobile stations that students could use in the hallway. I taught students how to use the *TouchCast Studio* app on their iPads and iPhones. They then became "ambassadors" to their other classrooms, charged with helping their teachers with the use of the app, and assisting their classmates as well (I conducted a Professional Development session for the entire staff before this experiment).

All one needed to do was observe the gleam in these new student leaders' eyes when they returned to my classroom throughout the school year, saying things such as, "Can we borrow two green screens," or, "My teacher needs help with our project. You don't have to come; I've got this." These ambassadors helped to change the climate of the entire school and caused many apprehensive teachers to get on board.

Ready, set, go green!

Before you throw out the "how much does this cost" question, think about this — I started with green screens from my Creative Arts Coordinator and eventually discovered other educators who were using all types of green material: construction paper, tablecloths, flat bed sheets, green fabric, and even found others who actually painted a wall green! With the use of science fair display boards covered in green, each student can have their own green screen recording booth! So, high budget, low budget, or no budget - let your creative mind go to work.

Tips for a smooth start

- If your school does not use iPads, digital cameras will work just as well.
- Check with your Tech Support Team for help getting set up correctly.
- Test everything yourself *before* introducing this to students. Where will you place your green screen? Are all devices working properly? Is the app/software downloaded onto all devices?
- Although I use *TouchCast Studio* extensively, there are other software and app options available that you will discover as you dig deeper.

The remainder of this chapter will focus on my use of the *TouchCast Studio* app in conjunction with my classroom setup. Ready? Let's go!

Before, during, and after

BEFORE the school year gets too far along, here are a few ideas to get students in front of a green screen and help them get to know each other:

1. Introducing…Me!

Classrooms are filled with students from right around the corner, as well as from around the world. Have students save images to their devices showing where they were born. Use maps and actual places. Do they know the city, state, country, or the hospital? Use those images to record or present a live version of "All About Me."

2. When I go to college...

To promote College and Career Readiness, tell students that they have been given a 4-year college scholarship, but they must narrow their selection down to their top two colleges. While students research, have them save images and videos of college campuses and campus life. Have students select their top two and then use those images/videos, placing themselves as the "new kid on campus."

3. Here I am, a professional...

The next great soccer player, NASA's leading female scientist, an IT specialist–the sky's the limit! Let students find images of someone currently working in their dream career. Have students use the green screen to transport themselves and stand next to their "career idol." This activity can stand alone or can be used as part of a unit on careers.

4. My progress report...

I suggest having students create an electronic portfolio, using readily accessible software such as Google Drive. If you use Google Classroom, the organizing of projects is a cinch, and sharing with teachers and peers becomes seamlessly integrated. All projects can be revisited later in the school year, or lead to extension ideas.

Remember, the **BEFORE** objective is to get students comfortable using green screen technology. It also allows teachers to identify quick learners and develop group leaders for future collaborative projects.

DURING the school year, look for ways to transform assignments into green screen presentations. Students' ideas will flourish as they continue having fun using green screens. Here are some seed starters to help you get going:

- Show students examples of news broadcasts or business shows where hosts are using maps, charts, or graphs projected onto a green screen.
- On the *TouchCast Studio* app, allow students to explore the Annotate (Maps, Images, Videos, Web Pages or Files) templates. These are valuable tools for *all* classrooms.
- Couple this technology with apps such as *Nearpod* that allow student work to be projected to the class from their seats.
- After allowing students to explore the *TouchCast Studio* News Studio and Talk Show templates, have students work as partners or in small groups and record a "show" discussing a **Reading English Language Arts** assignment or present "breaking news" about a **Social Studies** concept.
- Students can be interviewed while explaining their **Science** project with an appropriate image or live video background of them at work in the lab.
- **Creative Arts** students can record themselves completing a charcoal drawing assignment and then use the video for their green screen background as they discuss the steps it takes to complete their drawing, thus demonstrating an understanding of the concept taught.
- Let's get physical! Place **PE** students, learning the art of dribbling a basketball, onto the court of

their favorite team. Working with a partner, students can record each other as they learn the skill, and turn in their finished project for a grade.
- **ESOL,** anyone? Learning new words becomes fun in front of a green screen with a background of the student's country, and images representing words in their new language.
- Here's my **BIG ONE**!!! The STRETCH! What if getting students comfortable talking in front of a green screen translated into greater success with those dreaded Brief Constructed Response questions on state assessments? In my professional opinion, I believe this technology can make a difference!

I could go on and on, but this is where your creativity takes the baton!

Remember that the **DURING** objective is to get students and teachers continuously thinking of ways to transform lessons into audio and video enriched experiences.

Will this fit every lesson? No. Will every student get in front of the green screen? No. Will every student be engaged? YES! Many students have turned into classroom directors, camera operators, stage managers, and more. Remember, not all great Hollywood directors are former actors or actresses. We are helping them build new skills, and demonstrate a clear understanding of the 4 Cs: Communication, Collaboration, Creativity, and Critical Thinking.

AFTER students have become confident users of green screen technology, I offer a few suggestions:

1. Identify advanced users and assign them the task of training new students who transfer in during the school year.
2. Meet with the class and present a lesson or unit objective. Ask students to brainstorm ideas on how to accomplish the objective(s) using the green screen setup. This should increase student engagement and generate higher levels of enthusiasm among students.
3. Require partners or teams to:
4. plan their projects first.
5. share with you (The Executive Producer) their idea.
6. obtain your approval before starting.

Excited students using green screens can easily turn into groups sitting around chatting and exhibiting off-task behaviors. Accountability before projects begin can help maintain focus.

Try a "Previewing Session" where students show previews of their projects to the entire class, describing their progress to date. This can force accountability and add a little friendly competition.

YOUR MISSION, should you decide to accept it, is to make it possible. To do so:

1. Start small
2. Have fun.
3. Let the students do the driving!

MAKERS IN SCHOOLS:
ENTERING THE FOURTH INDUSTRIAL REVOLUTION

Working with green screen technology is something that I thoroughly enjoy, and watching student creativity grow and develop is what it's all about!

MICHAEL DUBOSE

About the Author

Michael DuBose is a Music Technology Educator, Composer, and Workshop Presenter. His musical journey started as a kid growing up in Motown. From Cass Technical High School in Detroit, to Tennessee State University, then on to Illinois State University and Northwestern University's School of Music; the quest produced a Bachelor of Music, a Bachelor's in Music Education, and a Master's degree, specializing in Music Technology, Arts Integration, and Composition. Workshops, lectures, and performances have been shared with audiences in the U.S., London, and Japan, celebrating the joys of learning music with children and adults. He is currently serving as a Creative Arts Technology Specialist in the state of Maryland where he resides with his wife Demetria and their three children.

Reach out with your questions and workshop requests. (michaeldubose4musictechnology@gmail.com).

COLOR ME HAPPY

Katie J. McNamara

After the excitement of embracing a makerspace simmers down, many are overwhelmed with what to purchase, where they will get a budget, and what will be successful. High-tech makerspaces are not the only options. A powerful, nearly free option exists: a coloring makerspace.

The school day has become more and more intense for students. Faced with multiple demanding classes, many students stay up past midnight working on homework and studying for tests. All too common in the lives of secondary students. These children have little to no downtime to relax and just be. They need a moment to be calm, a moment to regroup.

Even without the luxury of time, students deserve time to relax. Staying in a state of high stress, often due to " increasingly busy schedules, academic challenges, and concern for their future after high school " (Mueller 2018), actually prevents them from doing their best in the very classes to which they have dedicated their childhood. In the rush to prepare children for the next level, they are short on time to be children. They are cheated out of a task that has many rewards for the colorer as well as those they share time and space with.

Value

Initially, a color makerspace may be dismissed as babyish or preemptively thought of as something students would not even participate in. However, stress is real for every age. Coping with stress and preserving mental health is a valuable life skill.

Stress comes for our students from many different directions. Student stress doesn't only come from the need to perform well in academics and sports. According to Bo Paulle, sociology professor "chronic stress doesn't just happen to privileged, wealthy kids—in fact, its effects are likely most pronounced on the upper and lower extremes of the socioeconomic ladder." Basic survival becomes another set of stressors often impacting low-income schools and families. These may include safety, food, clean clothes, and even where they are sleeping for the night. Parent involvement adds another layer: Is the parent over-demanding of what they deem successful? Does the parent require financial assistance? Is the parent available?

Any element of stress creates a juggling act of surviving school. Students need coping strategies to keep stress from elevating into anxiety or depression. Some successfully implement a digital or physical planner. Knowing when deadlines are helps, but does not completely erase all stress. Healthy outlets become a necessary strategy.

A low-cost solution

Participating in a seemingly mindless activity, such as coloring, is far from mindless. In fact, students enter a state of mindfulness and even meditation without intentionally trying. The calming one gains from coloring seeps into them. Children who are calm usually make better, more rational decisions.

When coloring, there is no wrong choice. Our teenagers can choose pink, green, or aquamarine. They can stay in the lines; they can break every rule. There are no rules.

They can relax and just be. With a color in their hand, they find a new power: a power to chill and just be. Unbeknownst to them, they experience a peace associated with mindfulness. Almost intuitively, they seek out more opportunities to color without even knowing mindfulness or meditation, but knowing the euphoria of peace.

I have noticed that many students ask to borrow colors for school projects. Crayons, once a staple like milk and bread, are non-existent in many homes. Older siblings sometimes ask me to take a coloring page home as a way to connect with siblings.

For secondary students, the few minutes between classes that sometimes include walking across campus is not enough to regroup and have the proper mindset conducive to learning. They need something more. Even just a few minutes coloring, helps to provide a fresh slate that re-energizes students for the next class.

Coloring lends itself to a myriad of situations, being something one can do quietly in isolation and reap a voyeur escape. Coloring can supply solace in solitude. One can be alone in contemplation, or not, regarding the next color to use to create. One can be alone with the dragon or trees they bring to life.

Coloring can also be a silent group effort of accomplishment:

MAKERS IN SCHOOLS:
ENTERING THE FOURTH INDUSTRIAL REVOLUTION

If students' version of calm demands a bit of socialization, coloring can supply that, too. They can color beside friends. The conversation topic may vary; however, the relaxation of coloring remains constant.

Even as adults, many seek out the opportunity to create and socialize. Often the creation desired doesn't demand much thinking, an opportunity for one to near mindlessly fill in the white space. This desire is a reason why paint nights are popular.

Being creative and making something gives a sense of accomplishment. Everyone benefits from little moments of affirmation, that "yes, I did something."

How to begin

To get started, have a selection of two to four coloring pages. Keeping the selection small minimizes the stress of making a choice. Tugend (2010) notes several instances of too many choices simply being overwhelming and, "...an excess of choices often leads us to be less, not more, satisfied once we actually decide." However, offering more than one selection enables the victory in making a choice. Have a bin of colored pencils, crayons, or thin markers available. Place these colors by the papers; don't make students have to ask. They will naturally help themselves to the station.

Additional tips:

MAKERS IN SCHOOLS:
ENTERING THE FOURTH INDUSTRIAL REVOLUTION

- Let students find coloring pages
- Empower students to make coloring pages
- Keep your age group and likes in mind
- Supply "fun" coloring options (glitter pens)
- Colors will disappear; it's okay
- Post creations

Shake it up:

- Cover table with butcher paper
- Find pages that connect with content
- Make crayons

Color has power. A splash of color on a once white wall can bring smiles for years. Even color on toenails fills one with happiness. (Mine are currently purple.) The basis of a makerspace is to empower students to explore and create. A coloring makerspace definitely supplies that foundation. With a little more....that same space inspires collaboration and contribution. Most importantly, they will color themselves happy.

About the Author

Katie is a Future Ready Teacher Librarian that loves learning and trying new things to engage, empower, and excite other teachers and students. An ambassador of literacy and innovation, she enjoys inspiring and empowering others to be innovative and global digital leaders. She often shares her tech-infused programming ideas and activities via social media – including Twitter, Snapchat, and more – both amplifying students' voices and modeling effective uses of tech tools with other educators and librarians.

She currently teaches at North High School and Fresno Pacific University. She is an active global, national, and regional presenter and conference organizer for organizations including California School Library Association, KernCUE, CVCUE, EdCampVoice, and Ed Change Global. Additionally, she serves on Kern Council Teachers of English (KCTE), is a MackinTYSL Advocate, and #calibchat co-founder.

Create. Inspire. Empower. Repeat.
She is also a proud boymom.

ADDENDUM
(WHERE SHALL WE GO FROM HERE?)

Susan Brown and Barbara Liedahl

You are invited to engage with us moving forward! We encourage you to contribute to our living documents. Share your ideas and websites and blogs you own or visit often. See what others have contributed. Make connections.

Makers' Bibliography and Curation

http://bit.ly/makersbib (Submit on Google Form)
http://bit.ly/MakersShare (View on Spreadsheet)

Maker Book Website

http://bit.ly/makerbooksite

OTHER EDUMATCH BOOKS

This book challenges the thought that "teaching" begins only after certification and college graduation. Instead, it describes how students in teacher preparation programs have value to offer their future colleagues, even as they are learning to be teachers.

The Fire Within: Lessons from defeat that have ignited a passion for learning is a compilation of stories from amazing educators who have faced personal adversity head on and have become stronger people for it.

Follow *The Teacher's Journey* with Brian as he weaves together the stories of seven incredible educators.

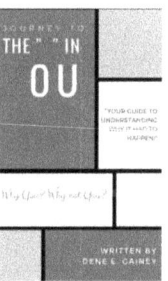

Through the pages in this book, Dene Gainey helps you gain the confidence to be you, and understand the very power in what being you can produce.

www.ingramcontent.com/pod-product-compliance
Lightning Source LLC
Chambersburg PA
CBHW061318040426
42444CB00011B/2703